Managing the Whirlwind

Patterns and Opportunities in a Changing World

By Michael H. Annison

MANAGING THE WHIRLWIND

PATTERNS AND OPPORTUNITIES IN A CHANGING WORLD

Author:
Michael H. Annison
President
The Westrend Group
P.O. Box 200335
Denver, CO 80220
(303) 321-6211

Published by:
Medical Group Management Association
104 Inverness Terrace East
Englewood, CO 80112
(303) 799-1111

Medical Group Management Association (MGMA) publications are intended to provide current and accurate information and are designed to assist readers in becoming more familiar with the subject matter covered. MGMA published *Managing the Whirlwind* for a general audience as well as its members. Such publications are distributed with the understanding that MGMA does not render any legal, accounting or other professional advice that may be construed as specifically applicable to individual situations. No representations or warranties are made concerning the application of legal or other principles discussed by the author to any specific fact situation, nor is any prediction made concerning how any particular judge, government official or other person who will interpret or apply such principles. Specific factual situations should be discussed with professional advisers.

Dedicated to Patsy, Elizabeth and Julia

TABLE OF CONTENTS

DIMENSIONS OF CHANGE
PREFACE

"This is a story without end. The most promising words ever written on the maps of
human knowledge are 'terra incognita' —
unknown territory.**"**
— Daniel J. Boorstin[1]

There were clear expectations when I was growing up in the
1940s and 1950s. Children would grow up, go to school, finish
high school and possibly college, find a job, get married, have
two children and live happily ever after. World War II had just
ended, the housing market was strong and jobs were plentiful.
John Kenneth Galbraith captured the spirit of the times in his
book, *The Affluent Society,* subtitled *The Economics of the Age of
Opulence.*[2] Given the allied victory in World War II and a national
feeling of optimism, there was every reason to believe our lives
would be predictable, orderly and successful.

When I was growing up in New York, I used to shop at the
neighborhood grocery store for my grandmother. I can still
remember watching the clerk reach for items from the high
shelves behind the counter. The grocery store has changed.
Today, I do my grocery shopping at the local King Soopers — a
large supermarket chain. I also buy flowers there, get prescriptions filled, get cash from the automatic teller machine (ATM),
buy ski lift tickets, rent movies and have breakfast. King Soopers
sells lottery tickets and has a shoe repair service, a post office,
an airline ticket counter and take-out Chinese and Italian food.

Having children is also different now. When my wife Patsy was born in 1940, my mother-in-law was in the hospital 10 days and the cost of delivery was $35. The hospital room was $3 a day; the delivery room $5; and the laboratory work $1. When my daughters Elizabeth and Julia were born in the late 1970s, Patsy was in the hospital three days and the cost was about $2,000.

These changes and countless others touch each of us. They affect our families and our relationships. They also affect our jobs and our organizations as well as how we get health care, educate our children and do our banking.

I wrote *Managing the Whirlwind* because I believe we can manage, rather than be victimized by, the changes we experience. I chose the book's title because the whirlwind is a useful metaphor for our times. All too often we are so caught up in the pressures of the moment that we have difficulty understanding the meaning of change. The harsh reality is that people who don't pay attention to change become lost in the whirlwind — often unnecessarily. Steel workers pressed for higher wages and benefits in the 1960s and, as a result, many were unemployed in the 1980s. Similarly, in the 1950s auto company executives ignored foreign competitors who by the 1980s controlled almost one third of the United States market.

On the other hand, people who take the time to understand and manage change usually prosper. The founders of Federal Express, Apple Computer and MCI Communications were willing to deal with change and work toward creating a different future. They realized the question wasn't whether there would be change, but how they could manage it.

Over the last decade as a business consultant, I have given speeches, conducted retreats and worked with clients in a wide variety of fields. In one way or another each assignment has focused on three issues:

■ What patterns and ideas underlie the changes we all experience?
■ What will the future look like? What changes will we have to deal with next? and
■ How can we manage change? What should we do?

Managing the Whirlwind addresses these issues and suggests ways we can manage change successfully. Planners have an aphorism which holds that if you're going in the wrong direction, speeding up doesn't help. One lesson is already clear. Because many of the rules from the past no longer apply, doing more of what we've always done is a prescription for disaster.

◼ DIMENSIONS OF CHANGE

> "Dealing with change is a little like trying to fix a plane while you're flying."
> — *Anonymous*

People caught up in the pressures of daily activities tend to view the changes they experience as isolated events rather than as individual aspects of broader patterns. These individual events are never isolated occurrences, but always part of a pattern of change which has speed and pervasiveness as its two main characteristics.

Speed of change

The first characteristic of change is that it will occur at increasingly rapid rates. Our early ancestors lived in a world in which change occurred slowly over centuries. The phenomenon was described by historian Arthur Schlesinger who pointed out that our ancestors lived in an agricultural society in which the future was always very much like the present.

Beginning in the early 1800s, change occurred more rapidly. As we entered the 20th century, the pace of change continued to accelerate. Early in the century, some changes occurred over the course of a lifetime. My grandparents were born in 1900 and were three years old when Wilbur and Orville Wright flew their first airplane at Kitty Hawk, N.C. Before they died, both had flown on Boeing 727s and lived to see the airline industry become a global enterprise. It is difficult for younger people to remember that in the middle part of this century, Pan American Airlines was the symbol of America around the globe.

Soon changes began to occur over the course of a single generation. By the 1970s and 1980s, change had begun to occur within a half a generation or less. In 1980, long playing records dominated the music industry. By 1990, cassettes and compact discs had replaced them.

As if this were not enough, the rate of change continues to accelerate. In today's computer industry, it takes about 24 months to conceive, design, develop, manufacture, market and sell a new product, many of which will have a lifecycle of 18 months.

The spirit of this accelerated rate of change was captured by a securities analyst for the hardware industry who observed that you could not take an accurate picture of a Home Depot discount hardware store because by the time you had developed the picture, the store would have changed.[3] This accelerating rate of change means that the question we face isn't whether things will be different, but how they will be different and how rapidly they will change.

Pervasiveness of change

Change used to occur in individual fields and then spread slowly to other parts of the broader society — a pattern similar to dropping a pebble in a lake and watching the ripples slowly spread from the center. Now, it is as though 10,000 rocks were dropped in the pond simultaneously with waves overlapping and colliding everywhere.

The changes we experience affect our personal lives, our families, our organizations and governments around the world simultaneously. They also affect how we think about the world around us. Physicists debate string theory and quantum mechanics. Biologists debate evolutionary change and punctuated equilibrium. There are similar debates in the fields of economics, history and medicine.

This shifting nature of change means we need to think about its impact differently.

■ We will all live in a future different from the present. When we talked about change in the agricultural society, it pertained to issues that would affect our children and our grandchildren. Now the accelerating rate of change means that the different future we discuss is the future in which we ourselves will live.

■ Change has become a constant. Most of us were raised in a world we believed was fundamentally stable. There might have been occasional outbreaks of change, but things would then settle back into predictable patterns. Now, change is the constant and stability is the exception.

■ We all manage change. The speed and pervasiveness of change forces all of us, willingly or unwillingly, into the business of managing change.

Organization of the book

Part one of the book discusses issues with which we grapple everyday. The emergence of an information society (Chapter One) coupled with the increasingly rapid development of new technologies (Chapter Two) forces all of us to think differently about what we do. What used to be true for society's elite has now become true for all of us: intelligence and information have replaced physical strength as society's strategic resource. New technologies have had an equally significant impact. We tend to think of technology as things we can kick, touch or feel. This is an understanding which needs to change. The root word of technology is *technique* and the appropriate use of emerging technologies has as much to do with how we use them as it does with the tools themselves.

Chapter Three describes how the growth of the information society and the increasingly rapid introduction of new technologies have led to startling changes in the relationships between organizations and the people they serve. Until recently, we accepted the idea that meeting the organization's needs ought to come before meeting our own personal needs. Through the 1950s, for example, IBM executives went to work knowing they would be assigned to new jobs and move about every three years (prompting observers to joke that the company's initials stood for "I've Been Moved"). Now, IBM executives and managers in other companies as well are more likely to make decisions based on personal rather than corporate priorities.

Chapter Four discusses how organizations can more effectively respond to the needs of people they serve and focuses on how we can redesign existing organizations so they can survive and prosper in a changing world.

Chapter Five is about quality — the idea that we can develop superior and simpler systems to more easily meet people's needs. Our organizations and the systems we use have become so complex that few of us even understand how they work. The process of obtaining a home mortgage, for example, has 180 separate steps. The registration process in the American hospital is, as near as I can tell, beyond anyone's comprehension. The systems we developed to serve us now, in fact, control us.

Chapter Six concerns collaboration and the idea that we can no longer "go it alone." Our preoccupation with heroes and individual achievement is giving way to the understanding that we must work together to accomplish what needs to be done.

Part Two focuses on how we can manage changes that affect us now, as well as those that will affect us in the future. Chapter Seven, "Developing Foresight," describes how we can anticipate the future and Chapter Eight discusses ideas which will shape what we do in the future. Finally, Chapter Nine describes steps we can take to deal with the issues discussed throughout the book.

One underlying theme of the book is that there are no magic solutions to coping with the present or managing the future. Each of us individually will need to change and together we will have to redesign the organizations we have created. Our actions today, tomorrow, next week, next month and next year will define history for our grandchildren. We have extraordinary opportunities to shape that future. My hope is that *Managing the Whirlwind* will help us learn more about how we can create a future that reflects the best we can be.

Michael H. Annison
Denver, 1993

ACKNOWLEDGEMENTS

One of the themes of *Managing the Whirlwind* is that we all have to continue to learn and I want to thank the people from whom I learned a great deal as I wrote. Over the last 10 years, I have had the opportunity and privilege to work with clients in a wide variety of fields. The opportunities to test ideas and learn from how they were managing change were invaluable. I am especially grateful for the continuing relationship with **Dan Wilford** and the board and staff at Memorial Care Systems and the opportunity to work with **John Findley** and the staff at Findley Adhesives over an extended period.

Numerous friends took the time to review and comment on early drafts and their observations were invariably helpful. These included **John Findley, Allan Dumas, Wally Sundberg, John Maurer, Father Marion Hammond, Peter Johnson, Diane Moeller, Judy Call, Joann Burstein, Dr. Hugh Gilmore, Gordon Hawthorne, Alan Palmer** and **Darrell Young**.

Others helped me learn what was involved in actually getting a book published: **Gilian Jolis, Dean Coddington, Jeff Hallett, Mary Bugnon, Holly Near, Bill Ouchi, Fred Ramey** and former Colorado Governor **Richard Lamm** were all supportive and instructive concerning the publishing process.

Still others helped with the editing and writing of the book. **Olive Carlson, Alice Christie**, the **Rev. Nita Ridley** and **Bradley Laughlin** worked on early drafts. **Sandy Widener** completed the work and the book is much better for her help.

I owe a special thanks to **Dr. Warren Bennis** and **Scott and Anne Jones**. Warren Bennis, Distinguished Professor at the University of Southern California and author of *An Invented Life: Reflections on Leadership and Change*, was especially supportive. He is a distinguished and gracious person and I appreciate his assistance. Scott and Anne Jones were supportive of the idea of *Managing the Whirlwind* from the first time we discussed it years ago. Their willingness to talk about the ideas in the book and their constant support were more than a friend could expect.

I also owe a debt of gratitude to **Hal Prink**, Director of Education at Medical Group Management Association, who suggested that MGMA publish the book. I also appreciate the help of **Fred E. Graham II, Ph.D.**, Senior Associate Executive Director; **Dennis L. Barnhardt, APR**, Director of Communications, **Barbara U. Hamilton**, Library Resource Center Director; **Brenda E. Hull**, Communications Project Manager; and **Stephanie S. Wyllyamz**, Communications Specialist.

Thanks to **Sally Mageath** whose thoughtfulness and professionalism were invaluable.

Finally, without **Susi (Jan) Mariacher** there would not have been a book. She has, in ways that I will never fully understand, been able to support clients, manage The Westrend Group business and, in her spare time, do the research and other work necessary to complete what at times seemed an endless project. I owe her a debt of gratitude beyond what I can express.

PART ONE
PRACTICALITIES

e live at a moment in time when change occurs so rapidly we see the present only as it is disappearing from view. **99**

— *R.D. Laing*

THE SHIFT TO AN INFORMATION SOCIETY

CHAPTER ONE

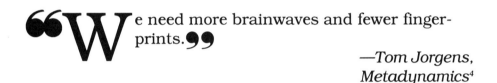

"We need more brainwaves and fewer finger-prints.**"**

—Tom Jorgens,
Metadynamics[4]

Inside ...

■ Characteristics of information

■ A shift in how we view time and resources

■ The impact of the information society

■ Living in the information society

■ THE SHIFT TO AN INFORMATION SOCIETY

> "You can put a 27 trillion dollar company together and there will be some fool on the corner outside who will have a better idea than you will. Head to head, he'll succeed and you'll fail."
>
> —*Barry Diller*[5]

Embracing new ideas is usually difficult. In the 1920s we struggled with the idea that the automobile represented a new technology rather than a fast horse — a difficulty reflected in our references to the first cars as horseless carriages. In 1938, Major John Kerr of the United States Army argued we shouldn't abandon "the tried and true horse" for unproven machinery.[6] This phenomenon shows up today in the difficulty we have accepting that the emerging information society is different from the industrial society of our past. The struggle is evident in how we think about the shift and, more specifically, in how we talk about jobs and the nature of work.

Most discussions about the information society have centered on the types of jobs being created rather than changes in work itself. The growth of jobs and businesses in the service sector is a visible and important part of the transformation we are experiencing. However, the more important issue is how work itself is changing. For the first time in history, intelligence — what we can think of as a combination of wisdom, experience, insight, cleverness and brains — has replaced strength as the primary determinant of success for all of us rather than just the social elite.

As Dr. Samuel Betances, a professor at Northwestern University noted, "Everything below the neck is minimum wage."[7] We now live in a world in which advances are made by those who out-think each other rather than by those with twice the money or twice the machinery.[8] In the information society, we all have to develop additional skills and work smarter. Iowa farmers still grow crops, but now, in addition to understanding farming, they also have to understand the effect of political and economic change in Russia on the Soviet ability to buy wheat. Accountants still prepare taxes and financial statements, but now they also need to understand strategic planning and organizational change. Accountants and financial managers have to learn how to measure what matters.

This shift to an information society affects chief executives, mail clerks and everyone in between. To be successful, we all need to know more and work more intelligently.

■ CHARACTERISTICS OF INFORMATION

> "Where does all the information go? What happens to it?"
> — *Dun and Bradstreet advertisement*[9]

Experience always shapes behavior and it has made us awkward in adapting to the emerging information society. We frequently retain an attachment to practices which may have helped us in the past, but are of little use to us now. As long as we manage information the same way we managed land in the agricultural society or money in the industrial society, we will inevitably have difficulty. The reason is that managing information is different than what we managed in the past.

Quality matters — not quantity

More may be better when we deal with land or money, but when we deal with information, quality matters, not quantity. When we manage information with the idea that more is better, we generate data that is duplicative or irrelevant. As Jeffrey Hallett, president of The Present Futures Group observes, we end up "glutted with data but starved for intelligence."[10]

The ongoing challenge in the information society is to learn how to substitute intelligence for mass.[11] In the industrial society, our problems were usually related to doing more of what we wcrc alrcady doing and we solved problems with more money or more people. In the industrial society, additional people added value. Now, additional people add cost and complexity. New employees take time from bosses and subordinates. They write memos (at the cost of $65 per memo).[12] They make phone calls. And, usually within a year or so, they maintain they are overworked and need an assistant.

> ... we end up "glutted with data but starved for intelligence."

In the information society we need better ideas and fewer people. When Safeway Corporation started stacking soap neatly on store shelves, sales increased five percent.[13] More product or more people didn't lead to increased sales — a better idea resulted in improvement. Continually searching for better concepts and methods to serve customers helped Findley Adhesives in Milwaukee increase sales by 20 percent, quadruple net income and reduce staff by 15 percent over a three-year period. An advertisement for Acura cars makes a similar point: "We don't think a car's cabin should be judged by the amount of ornamentation put into it, but by the amount of thought."[14]

Accepting the idea that less is better than more is key to managing information effectively. Most managers have two complaints about the information they employ. First, there is too much of it. They say that about 25 percent of the data they see is irrelevant or redundant. Second, managers frequently lack the information they actually require to perform their jobs. Some organizations have figured out how to address these issues. Oryx Energy, for example, once produced 4,603 reports a year — more than one for every employee. Employee groups went to work and identified the information they really needed to do their jobs. The result was a 20 percent reduction in the number of reports.[15] Similarly, the Celanese Corporation significantly reduced both the number and types of reports it produced.[16]

Another problem with treating information the way we treated resources in the past is that too much data leads to confusion. People bombarded with information can't tell what's important. The irony is that executives who complain that their people don't know what they are supposed to do usually created the confusion themselves. If employees aren't clear about what needs to be done, the fault lies with the managers. Reducing the amount of data we inflict on each other has two benefits. First, deciding what information is essential clarifies priorities and invariably leads to a second benefit — a reduction in the amount of data we collect, process, analyze, distribute and eventually discard.

Information cannot be "lost"

When we deal with tangible factors, we usually give up one thing to get another. This isn't true concerning information. When we share ideas and information, we give up nothing. We keep what we already know and often learn more.

Information is more valuable when shared

As we become more comfortable with the idea that information can't be lost, the next step is understanding that information is more valuable when it is shared because it helps us accomplish more than we could by ourselves. An understanding of this fact has fueled steady growth in both formal and informal mechanisms to share information. The growth of computer user groups, investment clubs and support groups, as well as the growing use of task forces, inter-departmental working groups, matrix management systems and dual reporting relationships within organizations all reflect a growing understanding of the need to move information across traditional boundaries.

One challenge is to share information within the organization. A second is to share it across entire organizations. For example, the National Basketball Association works with Digital Equipment to manage its scheduling system.[17] Also, a growing number of manufacturers and suppliers work together to simplify systems, design better products and reduce inventories.

Organizing work around separate professional specialties and independent organizations worked well in the industrial period, but these arrangements are now, at best, cumbersome. Organizations will have to become what Jack Welch, chairman of General Electric, has called "boundaryless companies."[18] They will need to eliminate barriers to learning and sharing information, whether within the organization itself or between the organization and the broader world around it.

Information and wealth

Finally, managing the information society is different because information and intelligence have now become our primary sources of wealth. In the industrial society, our primary assets were concrete. Now as Walter Wriston, former chairman of Citibank, argues, the source of wealth has changed, "Intellectual capital — the knowledge necessary to produce a product which produces wealth — has always existed. However, in the future, the ratio of intellectual capital to material is going to tip in the favor of intellectual component."[19] Charles McCall, president of HBO & Company, puts his finger on one of the challenges associated with this shift when he says, "It's hard to get used to the idea that your primary asset goes home at night."[20]

The consequences of this shift are real. Wal-Mart has replaced Sears as the nation's largest retailer, in part because Wal-Mart has developed methods to learn more about and respond to customers more quickly than Sears. Sears and Wal-Mart offer similar products but have different management systems. Wal-Mart has learned to substitute intelligence for mass, resulting in 20 percent lower overhead costs at Wal-Mart than at Sears.

■ A SHIFT IN HOW WE VIEW TIME AND RESOURCES

> "An invasion of armies can be resisted, but not an idea whose time has come."
> —*Victor Hugo*[21]

When we restructure a society, our views of time and what has value invariably change. There were significant shifts in what we thought had value when we made the transition from an agricultural to an industrial society. As summarized in the chart below, we are again making similar transitions.

Table 1
Society's changing characteristics

	Agricultural society up to 1850	Industrial society 1850-1950	Information society 1960 – ?
View of time	Past	Present	Future
Strategic resource	Land	Capital	Information
Transforming resource	Physical energy	Processed energy	Intelligence

Time

Our preoccupation with the present was appropriate during the industrial period, however, it causes problems in the information society. Quarterly financial statements, for instance, compel organizations to focus on the immediate present, often at the expense of the future. This preoccupation with the present makes it difficult to assess how individual events of the moment fit into broader patterns of change. It is as though we saw only the middle of a movie with no sense of its beginning or end.

Another example of this preoccupation with the present is the tendency of organizations facing financial pressures to cut back spending in areas such as training, marketing and research — areas more properly understood as investments rather than costs. Our unwillingness as a nation to increase investments in education is another example of this same tendency. Living in the information society means we are going to have to look where we're going and think as much about the future as we do about the present.

Strategic resources

Strategic resources are those resources we need to be successful. In the agricultural society, the strategic resource was land. It was difficult to be a

> *...preoccupation with the present makes it difficult to assess how individual events of the moment fit into broader patterns of change.*

successful farmer if you didn't have land. In the industrial society, the strategic resource was capital. Growing organizations required capital and, not surprisingly, bankers, investors and underwriters replaced farmers and land owners as central figures in society. Information has now replaced capital. While capital is still obviously important, it is intelligence that determines success.

Changes in the nature of strategic resources are significant because they determine how we arrange work and design our organizations. When a strategic resource changes, what needs to be managed also changes. As a result, arrangements that once worked now have limited effectiveness. During the transition from an agricultural to an industrial society, we redesigned our organizations to reflect the reality of a changed economy. We emphasized the importance of larger organizations and rearranged the flow of work around specialization: the idea that people would be more effective if they worked on only one aspect of the total business. The small family business was replaced by the much larger corporation. Because information has replaced capital, we once again need to redesign work and the organizations we have created.

Transforming resources

In the agricultural society, physical energy made it possible to transform raw materials into food and products. There were few machines; the cobbler used physical energy to make shoes just as the farmer used it to produce crops. In the industrial society, processed energy replaced human energy as society's new resource. Diesels, turbines and generators drove our industrial machinery. Now, the human mind has become the transforming resource. The importance of the shift is reflected in the comments of leaders such as James Baughman of General Electric and Robert Haas, chairman of Levi Strauss. Baughman comments, "You can only get so much more productivity out of reorganization and automation. Where you really get productivity leaps is in the hearts and minds of people."[22] Similarly, Haas argues that the responsibility of management is to help employees "tap their fullest potential."[23]

During the industrial society we equated capital and labor. Now the only thing an organization has that appreciates in value is the capability of its people. Everything else depreciates.

■ THE IMPACT OF THE INFORMATION SOCIETY

> "A man's mind once stretched never regains its original form."
> — *Oliver Wendell Holmes*

Redefinition of success and failure

During stable times definitions of success and failure are always clear. Success means performing activities correctly within well-defined boundaries and failure means making a mistake or stepping outside those boundaries. During times of turbulence, success and failure have very different meanings. Success is defined by how quickly and effectively we learn. This definition assumes that mistakes are a natural part of change. According to Bill Byrne, owner of 13 Taco John restaurants, "... I think I've learned more from my mistakes than my successes. You just pick up and go on; if one thing doesn't work, try something else. Never give up."[24] The definition of failure also changes. It is the moment at which there are no more options — there is nothing more we can do. For an organization, failure occurs when the organization itself ceases to exist. Until that moment, there are always possibilities. Certain times in our personal or professional lives will always be difficult. Success is measured by how effectively we deal with them.

Personal impacts

One of the subtle and important points about the shift to an information society is that success depends on our ability to continue to learn. The knowledge and skills that got us where we are were necessary, but are not adequate for future success. During periods of stability, we can apply what we have learned in the past to the present and future. During periods of change, we need to keep learning. All of us need to know more about issues such as quality, collaboration, innovation and organizational change, and, regardless of our job, we all need to know more about customer service as well as sales and marketing. Consistent with this idea, real estate agents, for example, are learning that their primary business is serving clients, not just selling houses.[25] Accountants are evaluated on how helpful they are to clients, not just their knowledge. During the industrial period, we could rely on professional skills to be successful. Now, professional capability is important, but success comes from being able to use our skills to help others.

We must also be aware of how relationships within organizations also change. Because intelligence has replaced strength as the primary determinant of success, women and men now compete on increasingly equal terms; in the not too distant future, men and women will be equal in fact as well as theory. Paying men more than women was common when physical strength was a paramount consideration, but now there is no justification for continuing discrimination.

Our difficulty in learning how to manage intelligence as a strategic resource is compounded by the fact that one part of the transition involves a changing understanding of intelligence itself.[26] In the industrial period, when we asked how smart somebody was, we were asking how well they knew the agreed upon rules. Now that the rules are murky, we are learning there are all kinds of intelligence. Some people learn by doing, others by reading, seeing or hearing. Each of us has different gifts and skills. In the information society, the question is not how smart someone is, but how are they smart — what skills, insights and capabilities do they bring to the task at hand and what can they contribute to building the future?

Organizational impacts

During the industrial period we developed and supported increasingly large organizations because they were able to develop products and services that made our lives easier. These large organizations become so much a part of the landscape that we tend to forget that in their early years they, too, struggled. As we undertake their redesign we tend to underestimate their earlier accomplishments. As a nation, we survived two world wars and at the same time provided jobs for a growing population. We educated growing numbers of children, improved health care and worked toward achieving the American dream of every family owning a home. We found ways to provide vegetables on a year-round basis and manage the temperatures of our homes and offices.[27] Beyond these tangible successes, our country continued to move (albeit painfully and slowly) toward ensuring equal opportunity for our citizens whether they were male or female and regardless of their race, color, religion, background or sexual preference.

While the organizations we created have enabled us to accomplish a great deal, we are now redesigning them to accommodate the realities of a changing world. Our efforts to date have been organized around three approaches. First, we are redesigning existing institutions. One aspect of this redesign has to do with how we handle information. In the past, information was generally available only to top managers who then provided subordinates with specific instructions. Today, we are learning the importance of providing information to people who need it, rather than hoarding it and then telling them what to do. Some managers still have difficulty understanding that their job is to ensure that appropriate decisions are made, rather than to make decisions themselves. At the same time we are eliminating staff positions and layers of management which have now become impediments to learning about and moving information. These are beginnings. But as David Kearns, the former Under-Secretary of Education and chairman of Xerox, has pointed out, we still have no idea of how much more we need to change.[28]

A second approach which can have a positive organizational impact is based on the idea that we can use what can be thought of as intermediary organizations much more effectively. In an information society, intermediary groups such as associations are increasingly useful. They enable members to share ideas and work that could not be as effectively accomplished relying solely on their individual resources. The Gas Research Institute (GRI) and the Electric Power Research Institute (EPRI) are important examples because they enable their member companies to undertake projects that are too risky or too expensive to be undertaken alone. Other intermediary groups enable participants to address issues which transcend traditional professional or organizational boundaries. The Business Roundtable, The Healthcare Forum and the Institute for Educational Leadership are models of organizations that bring business people, professionals and public sector leaders together to work on issues that affect each of them, but also cut across traditional boundaries.

A third variation of this technique involves the growing importance of organizations which may have been around for a while but are now more important than they were in the past. The new prominence of "think tanks," which were of passing importance in the stable industrial society, is one example of changing organizational relationships. Now, think tanks focus on the implications of change and as a result have reached an increasingly attentive and vastly expanded audience. The framework for many of our public policy debates has been shaped by established groups, such as the Brookings Institute, or newer groups, such as the Heritage Foundation. The Special Libraries Association (SLA) is another example. SLA is made up of people who seek out, organize and analyze information. Their role was secondary in the industrial society but is now increasingly important.

We are also creating mechanisms to meet needs and respond to new opportunities. In the academic world, colleges and universities have begun developing institutes or centers to assemble scholars who may come from different disciplines but share common interests. Many of the issues we face now cut across traditional academic boundaries. One suspects these new mechanisms may embody the principles around which we will organize universities in the future.

Similarly, we are creating new mechanisms in the private sector. Dell Computer applied the principles of direct mail to the computer industry. Also, home shopping networks on cable television employ the media to neatly sidestep traditional retailing.

■ LIVING IN THE INFORMATION SOCIETY

> "Our challenge is to work smarter not harder."
>
> — *Anonymous*

During the industrial period, our behavior was based on the idea that existing institutions were permanent and that what we learned in our youth would be useful throughout our lives. The emergence of the information society means that neither of these ideas are valid. To be successful in the information society, we need to think and act differently.

Learning and investing in ourselves

The idea that what we learned in our youth would be useful throughout our lives now has to give way to the idea that we need to continuously learn. People who rely on old skills to solve new problems are of little use in helping us manage the present or create the future. Because our ability to shape the future is a direct function of our willingness to learn more than we already know, each of us needs to have a plan for our ongoing personal development.

The 5 percent rule

Harry Hutson of Dennison Manufacturing has a companion rule for organizations: Successful organizations spend 5 percent of their gross income on the training and development of their people.[29] Again, in the information society, people are the only asset we have that appreciates in value. Only people can acquire new skills, embrace new ideas, see new opportunities and, with appropriate support, work more effectively.

Managing information

Because appropriate information is increasingly important, each of us needs to reassess the usefulness of the information we use. One problem of existing information systems is that they frequently measure results that no longer matter. It's bad enough that much of the information we collect and distribute is irrelevant; even worse, the money we spend on it is wasted. Managing information effectively dictates that we distribute only the information that is important so that everyone understands what the organization is trying to accomplish as well as their own individual roles.

Financial management

Financial statements are an especially good example of how the information we use is tied to the past rather than the present or the future. During the industrial period we equated capital and labor and this idea shaped how we developed financial systems. Because labor and capital were equated, financial statements treated all costs as if they were the same. Labor and capital may have been interchangeable in the industrial society, but not now. Traditional accounting systems hobble rather than help and we need to redesign them. Now, rather than all costs being the same, there are three types of expenses we need to manage. The first can be thought of as normal operating costs — costs that are a necessary part of running the organization. These include rent, utilities and heat. The second category combines the cost of items that decline in value, such as equipment, machinery and computers. Third are costs for research, training and development which we now need to understand as investments rather than costs.

To be successful in the information society, we have to:

■ reduce operating costs;
■ reduce expenditures for things that decline in value; and
■ increase spending in areas that now should properly be understood as investments rather than costs.

This means we have to redesign our financial systems so we can analyze and manage different kinds of costs rather than treating them all as if they were the same. The organization that cuts 10 percent across the board usually gets into trouble. The organization that finds ways to decrease spending on operating costs and items that decline in value, while increasing investments in training, research, development and marketing, is on the right track. If the information society really were an extension of the industrial past, none of this would matter. The fact that it isn't is the reason we have to change.

TECHNOLOGY AND TECHNIQUE

CHAPTER TWO

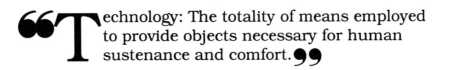

"Technology: The totality of means employed to provide objects necessary for human sustenance and comfort.**"**

— *Webster's Dictionary*[30]

Inside...

- Characteristics of emerging technologies

- Patterns of development

- Challenges

- Next steps

■

■ TECHNOLOGY AND TECHNIQUE

> "In two years most of our business will come from business areas that don't exist today."
>
> — *Jeffrey Kalb,*
> *Maspar Computers*[31]

During the 1950s the British mathematician Alan Turing argued that Europeans should play a leading role in shaping developments in the then infant computer industry. Aside from obvious economic benefits, Turing argued that if Americans were allowed to lead in the development of the industry, they would be preoccupied with computer hardware and insensitive to the machine's social implications.[32] Turing's assessment was accurate then and probably is now.

The reality is that the word "technology" has as much to do with how we arrange ourselves to use the tools we create as it does with tools themselves. The problem is that our preoccupation with things we can kick, touch and feel, coupled with traditional working arrangements, makes it difficult to take advantage of emerging technological capabilities. Too often, for example, we continue to use the computer as a fast typewriter rather than as a new and different tool.

On the other hand, the grocery store is one example of dramatic success in using new technologies. The electronic cash register, the shopping cart, the automobile and the computer have all been effectively integrated in the contemporary supermarket. The supermarket works because these individual tools are part of broader purchasing, financial and distribution systems that make it possible to stock stores and attract customers.

Each of these tools, even the lowly shopping cart, has been a part of revolutionizing the way we live. We have proven we can develop impressive tools. The challenge we face is to rearrange the way we work so we can use them effectively.

■ CHARACTERISTICS OF EMERGING TECHNOLOGIES

> "We may begin to see reality differently because the computer provides a different angle on reality."
>
> — *Heinz Pagels*[33]

The advanced computers and the other tools we are developing are qualitatively different from those of the past. Understanding their characteristics is essential if we are to use them effectively.

Technology and intelligence

One distinguishing characteristic is that emerging tools and technologies augment our intellectual, rather than physical, capabilities. In the agricultural society, the wheel and the plow amplified our physical capabilities. Machines and engines had the same effect in the industrial society. The difference now is that technologies being developed augment our intellectual capabilities.

One example is the work being done by the astrophysicist George Smoot at the Lawrence Berkeley Laboratory. Smoot and his colleagues have analyzed data generated by COBE (Cosmic Background Explorer) to explore the origins of the universe. Using computers, they were able to review 420 million measurements and detect variations of .000003 degrees from one part of the sky to another. Their research confirming the "big bang" theory of creation is described as "one of the major discoveries of the century."[34]

Because we hear large numbers (about the federal deficit, for example) on an increasingly frequent basis it's hard to absorb what they actually mean. Assuming the measurements could have been done at all, one researcher doing one measurement per minute and working 24 hours every day would need 799 years to accomplish what Smoot and his colleagues accomplished — assuming the researcher could have taken 420 million measurements without mistake.

The difference now is that technologies being developed augment our intellectual capabilities.

While Smoot's work represents an extraordinarily sophisticated application of new tools and technologies, the same principle underlies work many of us perform every day. Financial spreadsheet programs enable us to conduct analyses once beyond our capacity. Database programs help us analyze everything from our personal checkbooks to the results of marketing campaigns. Architects routinely use computer assisted design programs that enable them to see their ideas in three dimensions. Computers are increasingly useful in sports as well. Tony La Russa, manager of the Oakland Athletics baseball team, uses computers to analyze situations, trends and tendencies in his own team and his competitors.[35] The introduction of computers in auto racing has led to better designed cars that drivers can race more effectively.[36] In each case, the use of computers has enabled us to enhance our level of understanding of what we are doing and enabling us to substitute intelligence for mass.

These new technologies, especially computer and information technologies, have two impacts. First, they make it possible to understand far more than we could otherwise. Secondly, they make it possible to reduce or eliminate routine work that previously consumed much of our time.

Changing communities

When Winston Churchill observed that "we shape our institutions and then our institutions shape us,"[37] he could easily have been talking about new technologies and their effect on communities. In the agricultural society, communities were geographically defined. People generally lived, worked, prayed and played within limited geographic areas. In these earlier agricultural communities and even in small towns today, people know a great deal, sometimes too much, about their friends and neighbors.

Communities changed during the industrial period. The unity that characterized the earlier agricultural communities gave way to different and increasingly segmented relationships. We moved from the farm to the city and in the process the various parts of our lives which were once seamless were no longer interconnected. People left their homes to go to work and as a result relationships changed. We developed friends in the work place and different sets of friends where we lived. Once we knew a lot about the people around us; now we know most of them only in passing.

Emerging communications, transportation and information technologies have had two almost contradictory impacts. On the one hand, they make it easier for people to build relationships around common interests, even though they may be geographically distant. On the other hand, the same new technologies can also lead to increasingly isolated and self-contained communities that are frequently more interested in their own ideas and well-being rather than those of the larger groups of which they are a part. International corporations, for example, often have more in common with each other than they do with the countries in which they operate.

Similarly, national governments have an increasingly difficult time harmonizing the competing interests of groups with stronger commitments to their particular cause than to the broader common good. The hope is that we can learn to use new technologies to bring us together rather than reinforce existing more parochial interests.

Empowering people

Emerging technologies empower individuals in two significant ways. First, communications technologies dramatically expand the availability of information and as a result each of us is able to make decisions we once left to governments or large organizations. Cable News Network (CNN) coverage of the Persian Gulf War is a wonderfully symbolic example of how access to information enables citizens to make political judgments for ourselves rather than relying, as we did in the past, on governmental interpretations of events. During the Mideast conflict, reports from CNN's Peter Arnett were broadcast around the world in real time. Arnett's reports weren't filtered by either his own news organization or the heads of governments involved in the conflict.

On another level, the explosion of communication channels such as journals, computer bulletin boards, newsletters, magazines, television programs and radio shows also increases the capability to make decisions based on information we receive directly. The development of fiber optic systems, televisions with 500 channels and what is called a "national information highway" will further enhance our access to information. In this brave world of instant access to limitless information, the challenge is how we determine what matters.

Secondly, increasingly sophisticated tools and technologies have changed the relationships among people within organizations. Managers who came up through the ranks of the industrial organization had frequently done the work they supervised and, as a result, presumed they knew more than their employees about how it should be done.

The increasingly rapid introduction of sophisticated technologies results in managers often not understanding the work they supervise. In his book, *Liar's Poker*, Michael Lewis described how the Salomon Brothers developed real estate investment programs and pointed out that the firm's senior executives didn't fully understand the financial product opportunities that were not traditional stocks and bonds.[38] Similarly, computer-assisted manufacturing techniques are often better understood by the employees who use them than the mangers to whom they report. When employees know more about the work they do than their managers, the employees have more control of their jobs than in the past.

■ PATTERNS OF DEVELOPMENT

> "We have to provide twice the capability at the same price almost twice a year."
>
> — *Rollin Pampel*
> *Bull Information*[39]

Complaints about the confusion caused by the increasingly rapid introduction of new technologies is a good example of what happens when we get caught up in the pressures of a whirlwind. While the nature of individual technologies may vary and the rate at which they are developed differs, the underlying pattern is clear: all technologies get smaller, faster and cheaper. As a result, the relationships among people who use them has and will continue to change.

... all technologies get smaller, faster and cheaper.

Smaller technology

Emerging technologies invariably get smaller in one of two ways. First, they become smaller in absolute terms. In the electronics industry, vacuum tubes have been replaced by transistors and transistors in turn by micro processors. Each step has led to smaller components with greater capabilities. The first fully electronic digital computer — the ENIAC (Electronic Numerical Integrator and Computer) — built in 1946 contained 18,000 vacuum tubes and communicated with 2,000 flashing lights.[40] By today's standards it was a monster. New sub-miniature computer disks hold 64 million bytes of information. These bytes are equivalent of 32,000 pages on a device three and a half times the size of a postage stamp.[41] As another example of miniaturization, Robert Fischell, the chief of technology transfer at Johns Hopkins Applied Physics Laboratory (APL), points out that new developments make it possible to "put 10,000 transistors with 30,000 interconnecting wires on a quarter inch square that is 21,000th of inch thick."[42]

New technologies also make it possible to do more with the same mass. This represents a second version of technologies getting smaller. Changes in the design, materials, electronics and communications equipment on airplanes are examples of this phenomenon. Another example is the "smart highway," which contains optic fibers that record cracking, bending and stress, making highways easier and less expensive to maintain.[43]

Faster technology

Most new technologies, especially communications and information technologies, enable us to do more things much more rapidly. Prefabricated housing techniques reduce the time necessary to build new houses to as few as three days. The use of information technologies has dramatically speeded up manufacturing cycles: hand-held computers speed the check-in process at car rental agencies; electronic scanners speed the checkout process at the grocery store; and computers on cargo ships speed the unloading process by providing information for better scheduling.[44] In the steel industry, new technologies make it possible to produce a ton of steel in 1.5 manhours rather than the traditional five or six.[45] In these cases and others, the outcome is faster work.

Cheaper technology

New technologies not only get smaller and faster, they also become less expensive. Breakthroughs in the telecommunications industry have been so dramatic that a *Fortune* magazine writer observed, "If the automobile business had developed like the computer business, a Rolls Royce would cost $3 and go 100 million miles on a gallon of gas."[46] Even when the cost goes up, as it does, for example, in the cost of airplanes, the sophistication of the technologies being used leads to increases in value and capabilities that exceed the increase in cost.

The impact

The declining costs and increasing availability of new technologies dramatically alters the relationships between people and organizations. An important point is that because technologies get smaller, faster and cheaper, technological innovation augments our ability to do things for ourselves. The result is that we are less dependent on professionals and institutions. Accountants live with the reality that inexpensive computer programs enable clients to complete their own tax returns just as building contractors have to accept the fact that home owners can do many of their own repairs. In the past, real estate agents controlled information about houses for sale. However, as this information has become more widely available, people have been able to buy and sell their own homes.

The result is that organizations have to continuously rethink the products and services they provide. Organizations that continue to rely on their ability to do things for us will continuously lose ground to those that help their clients or customers do things for themselves.

■ CHALLENGES

> "Dealing with technology is difficult."
> — *Bruce Merrifield*[47]

The development of new technologies poses three significant challenges. One is whether existing organizations can effectively manage the changes required by new technologies. A second involves how we will handle ethical issues inherent in the development of new technologies, particularly in biomedicine and information handling. A third is whether we can safely manage inherently fragile, large technologies such as nuclear reactors and global computer-based information systems.

Can we adapt?

One of the difficulties in managing change is that the past always has a larger constituency than the future. It is easier to defend what already exists than embrace a different future. One example of these difficulties is the debate over the future of the New York Stock Exchange (NYSE). William Freund, chairman of the Economics Department at Pace University and a former chief economist at the NYSE, argues that because of information technology developments, "time is running out for the New York Stock Exchange."[48] Not surprisingly, this view is vigorously rejected by William Donaldson, NYSE chairman. Donaldson argues that "all that electronic stuff — machines talking to machines with no human in the middle — is about as realistic as airplanes taking off and landing without pilots. There are people who predict that someday it will happen, but I doubt it."[49] In fact, Donaldson has missed the point and his apparent inability to grasp the implications of information technologies for the NYSE raises the possibility that Exchange employees will join steel workers in the ranks of the unemployed.

A second difficulty in embracing new technologies is that using them enables us to do things which do not fit neatly into existing arrangements. One example of this challenge is the problem we have in categorization. Bruce Merrifield, former assistant secretary in the Treasury Department, points out that standard reporting systems, such as the OMB Standard Industrial Codes, are "hopelessly outmoded. Silicon chips and computer software are listed in a category of stone, glass and clay, and there is no code for biotechnology ... the bureaucrats are turning a crank that's 30 years old."[50] The problem is real and part of our challenge is to develop commonly agreed upon ways to talk about the tools we are developing.

Because new technologies will continue to be introduced at an increasingly rapid rate, another question involves whether we will look to new or existing institutions for their development. Our experience to date suggests that existing institutions have a significant commitment to preserve the present and this commitment makes it difficult, if not impossible, for them to create a different future. This question is whether companies like IBM can adapt or whether we will look to the Apple Computers of the world to create our future.

Ethical challenges

Because we now have the ability to design, alter and manipulate human life in ways unimaginable to earlier generations, developments in biotechnology, biomedicine and genetic engineering raise ethical questions that go far beyond concerns of the past. We can now replace just about every part of our bodies. Beyond this, we have developed a bewildering array of drugs that enable us to alter our minds. These developments compel us to think more about the fundamental nature of human existence: If we have replaced a person's organs and used drugs to alter his or her mental state, how do we determine what a "person" is?

On a more personal level, we all face painful questions about how to care for those we love when they are near death and the difficulty is reflected in debates about whether medical technologies are being used to prolong death or extend life. One example of the conflict is the debate over whether or not Dr. Jack Kevorkian should help others die using his "suicide machine."[51]

Emerging biomedical technologies raise ethical questions for organizations as well. Because employers can now screen potential employees for indicators of diseases, ethical questions center on whether organizations should be allowed to select employees based on what they might cost a company in health insurance claims.

Developments in information technology raise different, but equally serious, questions. One is how to maintain privacy in a world where personal information is increasingly accessible. When a market research firm analyzes my buying habits from store receipts, are they using information that is mine or theirs? What rights do I have about how the information is used?[52]

While we believe in the right of privacy, there are situations in which using private information may be in the public interest. Dennis Levine, a convicted Wall Street stock broker, parlayed

$38,000 into over $11 million using insider information and public telephones. Existing communications and computer technologies were available to monitor his illegal behavior, but the question is whether or not it would have been ethical to use them.

The debates on these and similar ethical issues have just begun. It will take years to develop the understanding necessary to reach any level of consensus. The harsh reality is that for the present we are forced to muddle through to the best of our ability.

Managing fragile technologies

There are continuing debates as to whether or not we have the capability to effectively manage some present fragile and/or dangerous technologies, let alone those we may develop in the future. Part of the problem centers on the idea that we should arrange new technologies in the same large centralized configurations we developed to manage older technologies. The breakdown at the Chernobyl nuclear plant which spread radioactive dust over parts of Russia and Eastern Europe serves as a symbol of our inability to manage such large and complex technologies. Similarly, the breakdown of AT&T's long distance computer system on Jan. 15, 1990, caused by a computer programming error, knocked out phone service for over 65 million people.[53] In both cases, our willingness to build large, centralized systems and to believe that nothing could go wrong led to disaster.

When we allow ourselves to be captivated by the tools and overlook the importance of the people who manage them, the result is inconvience at best and catastrophe at worst. When the Exxon Valdez ran aground in Prince William Sound off the coast of Alaska, the resulting oil spill caused hundreds of millions of dollars in damage to the state's wildlife, waters and economy. . A study by Consumers Union demonstrates that 48 percent of the credit reports it reviewed were inaccurate in some way.[54] In these cases and others, the problems were as much a function of human error as they were of the tools people used.

At issue is whether or not we can manage the technologies we have developed. Economist E.F. Schumaker was an early advocate of the idea that technologies should be organized on a human scale. The fragility of some of the tools we have developed is bringing us full circle back to the idea that we need to focus as much on people as on the things we can kick, touch or feel.

■ NEXT STEPS

> "You better be careful where you're heading because you just might get there."
> — *Anonymous*

Rushing to acquire and install new tools only compounds problems with using them. Paradoxically, going slower at the beginning enables us to move quickly once they are in place.

Involve people

People who will be responsible for the redesign of the systems associated with the introduction of new technologies have to be involved in determining which technologies will be used and how they will be incorporated into everyday operations. Too often we have invested in new tools without involving people who will use them and the not surprising result is they are either resisted or, in some cases, ignored.

Expand training

As the rate of technological change increases, training budgets have to increase. As mentioned, approximately 5 percent of gross income has to help people understand and learn how to use new tools.

Redesign work

Incorporating new technologies invariably leads to the need to redesign work. In order to use capabilities effectively, we have to remove barriers among different departments.

Assess future technologies and update products, services and markets

An accelerating rate of change means that every organization has to regularly assess the potential impact of emerging technologies. Successful organizations schedule regular planning sessions to focus on the implications of new technologies. Participants in these sessions are drawn from a diverse group of people who can bring the organization's best thinking to bear on questions about what may lie ahead. Chapter Seven discusses more about ways this can be accomplished.

In the stable past, the need to focus on emerging technologies was minimal compared to today. The technologies we are developing are not just additional tools to reinforce the way we've always done things, but rather opportunities to significantly redesign the way we work.

PEOPLE MATTER:
A CUSTOMER-DRIVEN SOCIETY

CHAPTER THREE

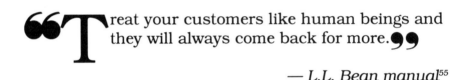 **T**reat your customers like human beings and they will always come back for more. **99**

— L.L. Bean manual[55]

Inside ...

■ People have choices

■ Rethinking products and services

■ Sales and marketing

■ Pragmatics: The value of people

■ What it takes to serve people well

■ PEOPLE MATTER: A CUSTOMER-DRIVEN SOCIETY

"The consumer is not a moron ..."
— *David Ogilvy*[56]

As mentioned earlier, one striking aspect of the industrial society was the extent to which we were willing to subordinate our personal interests to those of organizations. Customers, employees, investors and even communities were surprisingly willing to put organizational priorities ahead of personal needs. Customers were willing and even eager to trade in, replace or buy more of whatever companies produced, whether it was toothpaste, pet rocks or cars. The idea that business practices were worthy of emulation by others gained momentum early in this century and even today has broad support: leaders of nonprofit organizations, trade associations, school systems, hospitals and government agencies talk about the need to be more like business in how they conduct their affairs.

These attitudes are changing. Over the last several years, we have begun to demand more of our organizations and there is a growing belief that organizations should meet the needs of people they serve rather than the other way around. It is no small irony that many organizations may not be able to change rapidly enough to meet expectations they themselves helped create.

Every now and then there are events that vividly symbolize this change. Coca-Cola's experience when it introduced New Coke is a powerful example of the dramatic alteration in the relationships between organizations and the people they serve. Coca-Cola spent several years and millions of dollars developing New Coke. It took customers fewer than 90 days to overturn the company's decision. Coca-Cola realized it had made a mistake and, rather than try to defend it, reintroduced what is now called Coca-Cola Classic within 120 days. Coca-Cola customers showed how easily decisions made by one of the country's most successful corporations could be overthrown. Coca-Cola's chairman,

Robert Goizueta, captures the spirit of the experience when he observes that, "To be successful in the future, we must be willing to make what sells rather than sell what we make." In this instance, the customer, rather than the organization, controlled the market.

Coca-Cola is not alone in recognizing the importance of meeting the needs of people they serve.

- IBM used to dominate both its customers and competitors. Now Big Blue is running *mea culpa* advertisements stating that as the company gets older, its hearing is improving.[57] IBM is also saying it will encourage business with anyone rather than focusing only on its own systems and its terms.[58]
- According to Donald Petersen, former chairman of Ford, "If we aren't customer-driven, then our cars won't be either."[59] This observation is a far cry from the comment popularly attributed to Henry Ford: "They can have any color as long as it's black."[60]
- Xerox now tells its customers that it will replace any product for any reason within three years of the purchase.[61]
- Airlines, hotels, supermarkets and even car washes offer frequent buyer coupons to build customer loyalty.
- The California Angels baseball team stocks both men's and women's restrooms with diaper-changing tables. Its food service includes traditional hot dogs as well as sushi bars.[62]

This emphasis on meeting people's needs, rather than needs of an organization, represents a return to the values of the agricultural society. During most of the industrial period, our population grew so quickly that lost customers could be easily replaced. Economists tell us we never value what we have in abundance, and a growing population meant that regardless of what organizations said, their markets were both too large and growing too rapidly for individual customers to be important. That era is gone. Rising customer expectations, demands for individualized products and services and an increasingly competitive global economy have shifted our focus to meeting the needs of individual customers. In the 1990s, there is no such thing as a marginal customer — or a marginal competitor.[63] A company's individual customers are important for two reasons. First, because the rate of population growth has slowed, lost customers are no longer easily replaced as they were in the past. Second, lost customers are often an early sign of shifting markets.

Just as there are no marginal customers, there are now no marginal competitors. Japanese car makers, Federal Express and Apple Computer are examples of competitors ignored by American car makers, the post office and IBM. Rather than taking their once small competitors seriously and trying to learn from them, American car makers, the post office and IBM ignored them. The result led to significant changes in markets and who served them.

> *In the 1990s, there is no such thing as a marginal customer — or a marginal competitor.*

Now, consumers have choices — a fact that affects how they think about products and services, as well as how they are sold.

∎ PEOPLE HAVE CHOICES

> "Buying a pair of sneakers has now become a major intellectual exercise."
> — *Tom Atchison*
> *Atchison Consulting Group*[64]

Tom Atchison's comment about sneakers is a vivid illustration of the consumers' new power. In the past, a sneaker was a sneaker. Now we have walking shoes, jogging shoes, running shoes, athletic shoes for every conceivable sport, and hundreds of choices of color, height and sole designs. As Atchison wryly observes, now it takes a consultant and a bank loan to buy a pair of sneakers. This is also another example of why companies should not ignore marginal competitors. Converse used to monopolize a market now dominated by Nike and Reebok.

We also have and desire more choices where we purchase. We can buy plane tickets from an airline, American Express, a local travel agent or even the neighborhood grocery store. We can get credit cards from a bank, through an airline, the American Automobile Association, the Audubon Society, General Motors, General Electric, AT&T and even the Catholic church.[65] We can also easily substitute products and services. At The Westrend Group we can communicate with clients by fax, letter, overnight delivery, telephone or face-to-face.

We have similar choices in other aspects of our lives.

- We can shop using "800" telephone numbers, catalogs or home shopping networks on cable television. When we shop, we can purchase at boutiques, department stores, discounters or hyper-markets such as Wal-Mart stores.
- In financial services, our parents had checking and savings accounts, a home mortgage and maybe some stock. Now when we invest we choose from products such as options, reverse options, zero coupon bonds, euro-bonds, mutual funds, products with names like TIGERS, WINGS, DATES, CATS or libor-based floating rate notes.[66]
- When our parents were sick they went to a hospital. Now, depending on the situation, we can receive care in a hospital, doctor's office, urgent care center or out-patient clinic. We can also select among different types of health care, including traditional medicine, acupuncture, homeopathy and a growing number of other non-traditional medical approaches.[67]

The increasingly rapid rate of change means that customers will continuously expect new products and services to meet their changing needs.

The increasingly rapid rate of change means that customers will continuously expect new products and services to meet their changing needs. Companies will have to keep adapting to survive. The recent experience of the British banking system provides a telling study of how organizations learn to deal with growing competition. According to the *Wall Street Journal*,[68] "Not long ago, ordinary Britons practically begged their local branch managers for personal loans ... before, you weren't a customer, you were a supplicant." Now, British banks jockey with traditional and non-traditional competitors for the privilege of serving clients. Another illustration of adaptation is Britain's largest clothing chain's entry into the mutual fund business, targeting its 14 million customers. Additional rivals include foreign corporations such as Citicorp, Chase Manhattan and American Express, as well as British organizations such as the General Municipal Boilermakers and Allied Trade Union which introduced a Visa card to serve its 800,000 members. Like the rest of us, British bankers are learning to live in a world in which people have choices.

Organizations that continue business as usual will be hurt by this shift to a world in which people matter. Conversely, companies obsessed with meeting customer needs, rather than those of their own organizations, will thrive.

■ RETHINKING PRODUCTS AND SERVICES

"There's no such thing as a commodity."
— *Theodore Levitt*
The Marketing Imagination[69]

In the industrial society, the focus was on the product. Now, the focus is on the product in the context of the total relationship between an organization and its customers. The circle diagram that follows is one way to think about this relationship.

Figure 1
Products and Services

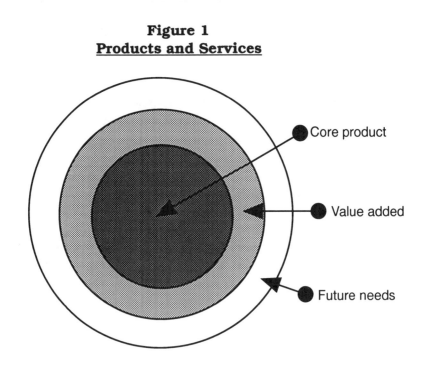

At the center of the circle is the core product or service: the grocery store sells food, the airline flies us from one city to another, or the real estate agent helps us find a house. In the industrial society, the product was the organization's primary and, in many cases, only concern. Industry boundaries were clearly defined, choices were limited and there was little need for companies to do more than provide their core product or service. Now, organizations that focus solely on this core product face difficulty because they compete with others who understand that the core product represents only one part of its total relationship with customers.

Given the choices available, consumers can always find organizations that do more than just provide core products. The second circle, representing added value, embodies dimensions of service that go beyond the product. This concept is illustrated by Midwest Express. This organization doesn't just fly people from one city to another. Every seat is first class and attendants make fresh chocolate chip cookies on every flight. Similarly, smart manufacturers spend time on billing systems, packaging and every other part of their relationship with customers.

Some organizations have already developed a corporate ethic focused on customers. Jan Carlzon, chairman of SAS Airlines, stresses the importance of each customer contact. He refers to "moments of truth" when he describes a SAS passenger who left his ticket at his hotel. The SAS agent promptly issued a new one and sent a messenger to retrieve the passenger's forgotten ticket.[70]

Barry Steinberg of Direct Tire goes far beyond selling tires. The waiting room at Direct Tire is immaculate: magazines are current, coffee is freshly brewed and there are plenty of windows. Loaner cars are provided to customers while Direct Tire works on their cars.[71]

Judy George, founder and CEO of Domain Home Furnishings, uses Polaroid cameras to give potential customers a photograph of the furniture they're thinking about buying. The salesperson writes his or her name on the back of the picture and suggests the customers see how the furniture will look in their home. The effect of helping people furnish their homes, rather than just trying to sell chairs and tables, has resulted in approximately a 25 percent increase in Domain's sales.[72]

The customer's future needs are represented in the third circle. Successful organizations focus as much on meeting future needs as they do on present issues. In the computer industry, developments such as voice-activated systems and computers that accept handwritten entries are examples of a focus on innovation and users' future needs.

The growing emphasis on meeting customer needs means companies have to do two things. First, insure that core products and services are high quality, because there is no longer any need for customers to tolerate shoddy products or services. Second, continuously find ways to improve their relationship with the people they serve, such as by providing added value and anticipating the customers future needs.

■ SALES AND MARKETING

"Ninety percent of American companies are
still not customer-driven."
— *Don Beveredge*[73]

Expanding customer choices and changes in how we think
about products and services have significant implications for
sales and marketing. Sales and marketing consultant Don
Beveredge has described four generations of salespeople to clarify
the difference between focusing on the product and focusing on
the customer.[74] The first generation is "good ol' boys"— appropri-
ately named in this case because they are usually male. These
are the Willie Loman's who sell to their friends. The difficulty
with good ol' boys is that their friends change jobs or die and
over time, their client base shrinks. The second generation is
what Beveredge calls peddlers. These are product pushers who
tell customers, "Here's what I've got, how many do you want?"
The problem with these two groups is that they never slow down
long enough to think about the customer's needs.

Salespeople in these two groups face problems because they
are competing with a third group — professional salespeople —
as well as the salesperson in the fourth group whom Beveredge
describes as a "sustaining resource." Because the sale is easier if
they know their customer's interests, the professional salespeople spend time with clients asking questions to determine if
the product or service will be helpful to them. The salespeople
Beveredge describes as "sustaining resources" know so much
about their customers that they are viewed as unpaid staff for
the customer's organization. As an example, at The Westrend
Group, Vicki Stevinson of Stevinson Design helps publish our
newsletter. From our initial conversations, she made it clear she
was interested in helping Westrend whether it meant doing the
work or teaching us how to do it. Her interest was in our well-
being, rather than her company. Meeting our needs meant she
would be successful. Similarly, Carol Gill of U.S. West Commu-

∎

nications is one of the best salespeople I've ever met. She asks questions rather than talking about cellular phones.

Organizations that focus on meeting people's needs are different from those that focus on products or internal operations. The organization focused on people emphasizes marketing which in the information society is defined as the ability to continuously redesign products and services so they meet customer needs. Service represents activities after the sale and has become increasingly important. It

> *In the industrial society sales and marketing were the responsibility of the sales force. In a customer-driven society, it is everybody's responsibility.*

includes the performance of the finance, packaging and shipping departments, all of whom have relationships with the customer.

In the industrial society, sales and marketing were the responsibility of the sales force. In a customer-driven society, it is everybody's responsibility. The leadership of the 3M Corporation, for example, insists that 25 percent of the company's income come from products that are fewer than five years old. All 3M employees spend 15 percent of their time thinking about new products and better ways to serve customers.[75]

∎ PRAGMATICS: THE VALUE OF PEOPLE

"The quality of the product is what the customer says it is."
— *James Balckon*[76]

The focus on serving people well creates a situation in which both the customer and the organization serving them thrives. The White House Office of Consumer Affairs estimates that the value of customer loyalty is:

■ Potential total revenues from a single customer in a life time of $140,000 in the automobile industry;
■ Profits of $80 a year from the average bank customer;
■ $2,800 in profits over a 20-year period for an appliance manufacturer; and
■ Total annual sales of $4,400 at the local supermarket.

These numbers suggest that serving customers well leads directly to increased income and profits.

We also know more about what happens when things go wrong, which is indicated as follows:

■ 96 percent of unhappy customers never complain about rude or discourteous treatment;
■ 90 percent or more of those dissatisfied with the service received will not return;
■ Each unhappy customer will tell his or her story to at least nine other people; and
■ 13 percent of those unhappy former customers will tell their stories to more than 20 people.[77]

Because the cost of obtaining a new customer is almost five times the cost of keeping an existing one,[78] companies can no longer afford to break faith with the people they serve. When Beechnut diluted its baby food,[79] people switched brands. The cost of replacing these customers was significantly higher than Beechnut doing what it should have done in the first place.

Frustrated customers — with voting power — passed Proposition 103 to regulate automobile insurance rates in California. Following the election, Gerald R. Maatan, president of Kemper National Property and Casualty, said the insurance industry had "to wake up to the fact that the public is frustrated by the high cost of auto insurance and blames us along with everybody else. The insurance industry spent a lot of money in California; but either we didn't get our story across or we were talking to an audience that didn't want to hear what we had to say."[80] Insurance companies spent $50 million in the campaign — and lost.

The election had the same symbolic value that Coca-Cola's experience did, but it's still not clear that insurance companies understood the implications of what had happened.

On the positive side, companies that support the people they serve are successful. For example, the Tattered Cover Book Store in Denver continues to grow because it has both an extraordinary range of titles and, more importantly, a knowledgeable staff committed to serving readers. The bookstore accepts checks without identification because it is easier for the customer, less expensive and less time consuming. Also, the staff can efficiently locate and order almost any book. In a totally different industry, cab drivers in cities such as Denver, Phoenix and Miami are being asked to dress neatly and go through training programs because, as Tom Murphy, who runs the Miami-based USA Nice Cabby training program, states, "Tourism is a high-stakes business."[81]

Another change smart companies are making involves the handling of complaints. When the focus is on the company, rather than the customer, a complaint is perceived as a criticism. Too many organizations respond that the customer is wrong or doesn't understand. This view is captured in the wry observations that schools would be wonderful places without children, hospitals would be great if it weren't for the patients, and retail stores would work well if it weren't for the customers getting in the way.

Organizations focused on the customer thrive on complaints because they are the least expensive and easiest way to find out what needs to be improved. The Marriott Hotel at the Minneapolis/St. Paul Airport hands guests cards at check-in which state that the Marriott will pay $20 if the hotel doesn't provide an easy check-in, clean room and an efficient check-out. All the guest has to do is hand in the card, tell the staff what went wrong and then receive $20. This straightforward approach is an easy and remarkably inexpensive technique to encourage customers to inform hotel employees how to improve. In an organization focused on people, customer complaints are opportunities.

■ WHAT IT TAKES TO SERVE PEOPLE WELL

"Decisions would be a lot easier if we just
remember what customers want."
— *Diane Thormodsgard*[82]
First Bank System

The emphasis on meeting people's needs is, in a very real
sense, a return to the values of a rural and agricultural society.
From this perspective, the development of the industrial society
and the growth of large organizations shattered the patterns and
relationships of that earlier era when merchants knew their
customers personally and most products were individually made.
Historian Daniel Boorstin has pointed out that until World War
I, most clothing was custom-made. The war changed that when
the requirement for large numbers of military uniforms in standard sizes led to mass manufactured clothing.[83] One part of the
work we have ahead is to blend the caring values of that earlier
period with the technological capabilities of the present.

Shifting perspectives

In almost every business learning to view what we do from
the customer's perspective rather than our own is both essential
and difficult. One common refrain, unfortunately repeated far
too frequently, is that customers "don't understand." Too often,
business people, educators, health care professionals and others complain that if the people they serve only understood, they
would be more supportive of the organizations that serve them.
Following this line of reasoning, if we "understood" we would
"buy American," support our schools regardless of their performance and be sympathetic of, rather than frustrated by, rising
health care costs.

The shift to a customer-driven society requires that we accept
James Balckon's idea that "The quality of the product or service
is what the customer says it is."[84] There will always be difficult

and unreasonable customers; but too many of us cite a few examples as the reason to ignore constructive suggestions from the thousands who are seeking improvement by requesting better products and service. One outstanding example of a product developed by listening to customers is Quicken — a financial management software package. Quicken staff members silently watch users work with the software so they can learn how to improve it. The purpose of watching customers isn't to tell them what they're doing wrong, but to learn how to redesign the program so it will conform to how people actually use it.

Another shift is the idea that meeting customer needs is a journey rather than a trip. On a trip, we travel from one place to another and stop. A journey, on the other hand, is continuous. People's needs and desires will always be changing. Therefore organizations will need to keep changing if they want to stay in business.

This shift in perspective can lead to dramatic changes in organizational behavior. In a customer-driven company, staff members spend more time with customers than with co-workers. Internal competition is based on how well employees meet customer needs rather than how well they play office politics. Personnel evaluations are based on customer observations in addition to supervisor's comments and managers willingly give up staff and financial resources to help other departments meet customer needs.

Understanding people we serve

A customer-driven society requires that everybody in the organization spend time with clients. In most organizations, working with customers is the job of those on the front lines — direct sales, customer service or community affairs personnel. Employees in research, manufacturing and finance are not thought of as having responsibilities to customers. Instead, they develop ideas, make the product or pay the bills. When professionals rarely see the people they serve they invariably develop tunnel vision and become preoccupied with their own jobs or the needs of their own department. In successful organizations everyone works with customers. This eliminates the phenomenon of people who never see customers telling others what customers really want. It also enables staff members from different departments to work together to compare ideas about customers and focus their energy on meeting customer needs rather than those of the departments or the organization.

Within an organization, everyone should spend time working with people in the departments they serve because it helps build an understanding of how what we do affects other people. For example, when research and development people help manufacture the products they design, the result is always better designed products that are easier to make.

Investing in what matters

Organizations that focus on customers will change the way they use financial resources. Investments in research and training or developing future products and services increase and overhead costs (general and administrative costs) go down. The percentage of total salary dollars spent on people who serve customers and those who directly support them increases. The percentage of salary dollars spent on people who are distantly related to customers declines. The goal is to meet the needs of the customer and plan for the future, not invest in the organization's overhead.

Organization rearrangement

Our present hierarchical systems were designed to reduce risk and enable us to produce standardized products. By any reasonable measure in the industrial age these arrangements were extraordinarily successful. However, now that the context within which organizations operate is changing, we have to again modify how we arrange our organizations. Successful businesses will deal with several issues differently.

■ Responsibility for customer service: managers will set overall goals and direction, but people who work with customers will have greater responsibility and authority to satisfy customers. 3M, for example, now has sales-people approve customer refunds on the spot. The company jettisoned it's elaborate approval process and gave the authority for approving refunds to people best able to make that decision.[85]

■ Cross training: in industrial organizations, which focused on producing standardized products, each person had one specific job. Now, to provide the flexibility necessary to respond to changing customer expectations, people need to be cross-trained. As workloads shift, organizations that support cross-training can respond to market changes and/or different work flows.

■ Fewer administrative levels: continuing change and the need to quickly respond to customer needs means that successful organizations will reduce management layers developed during the industrial period. Traditionally, large organizations used committees and management layers to ensure consensus for organizational actions. These arrangements now make effective response difficult.

These changes in organizational arrangements are the next natural stage in the evolution of the systems we've built. They represent sensible steps we can take to recapture the values of that earlier agricultural period and capitalize on our new capabilities.

QUESTIONS OF SCALE:
GETTING THE QUESTION RIGHT

CHAPTER FOUR

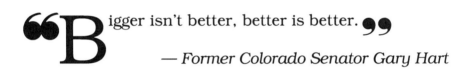

"Bigger isn't better, better is better. **"**

— Former Colorado Senator Gary Hart

Inside...

- Why organizations don't work

- Requirements for success

- Alternative arrangements

- Better ways of doing things

■ QUESTIONS OF SCALE: GETTING THE QUESTION RIGHT

"We may not be sure what the answers are
— but we do need to be sure we're asking
the right questions."[86]
— *Robert Kaufmann, Headmaster*
Deerfield Academy

Throughout the industrial period we embraced the ideas that bigger was better, and more was better than less and believed, for example, that big cars and large organizations were better than their smaller counterparts. In an information society we have to consider if these ideas are still useful. Many of us know people for whom "more," whether it was money, fame or power, caused more pain than satisfaction. There also are examples of people like the Rev. Jeb McGruder, who found more peace as a minister than he had known as a high-powered White House staff member involved in the Watergate scandal.

Our approach to organizational and industry questions of scale has generally been to focus on whether we should centralize or decentralize. The airline business is one example of an industry that has consolidated. Pan American, Eastern and Frontier have all gone out of business, while Delta, United and American have faced challenges, but continue to grow. Also, state and local governments have expanded their responsibilities in areas such as economic development and environmental regulation. Ernest Boyer, president of the Carnegie Foundation, summarized the challenge in education — and in other fields — when he observed, "What we are trying to work out now is a unique balance between local control and national results."[87]

Individual organizations wrestle with the same issue. ConAgra, Georgia Nekoosa, Wal-Mart and 3M Corporation are examples of very successful large organizations. At the same time, an argument can be made that the equally large IBM, Sears and General Motors would all be better off if they were smaller.

> *The question isn't whether we should centralize or decentralize, but rather how we should arrange ourselves to accomplish what needs to be done.*

The difficulty with talking about centralization and decentralization is that it focuses attention on the wrong issue for two reasons. First, they focus our attention on the organization structure and in doing so preclude talking about the organization's values, goals, future or ability to serve people. Second, debating questions about scale is a good example of letting ourselves get caught up in the whirlwind. We created large centralized organizations because we thought they could help accomplish what we wanted to do — not because they had any value themselves. Now we have become so preoccupied with an organization's size that we have lost sight of its purpose. The question isn't whether we should centralize or decentralize, but how we should arrange ourselves to accomplish what needs to be done.

Resolving many of our frustrations requires an understanding of why most large organizations don't work effectively and what needs to be done for them to be successful. We need to consider alternative organizational arrangements and better ways to accomplish what we need to do.

■ WHY ORGANIZATIONS DON'T WORK

> "It's hard to teach an elephant to dance."
> — *Anonymous*

Most of our existing organizations have developed characteristics which make dealing with change difficult, if not impossible. Focusing on scale muddies the water since organizational problems have less to do with size than characteristics such as: a desire for stability; slow decision-making processes; use of high-volume, rigid systems; a reliance on specialization and issues inherent in how information is managed.

Desire for stability

Many large organizations still use procedures originally designed to reduce risk, maintain stability and ensure continuing growth. One example is the use of committees. The original purpose for the development of committees was to reduce risk in the industrial organization. As organizations grew, committees were developed to ensure that no one part of the organization would impair the performance of another. Unfortunately, the committee structure is still with us even though its existence hampers our ability to exploit opportunities.

Multiple management layers have the same effect. Both multiple management layers and committees tend to focus on minimizing risk rather than maximizing opportunity. This desire for stability was appropriate when change occurred slowly over long periods of time. Now it represents a major stumbling block to success. Jack Welch, chairman of General Electric, is right when he says that organizations have to change faster than the world around them to survive. The challenge is to arrange ourselves to manage change rather than defend stability.

Slow decision making

Large, centrally run organizations are cumbersome. The desire for stability combined with the time it takes to reach decisions means they are slow to respond to customers, employees and the communities they serve. Over time, their policies and procedures have become so voluminous and complex that few people even understand them. The volume of paperwork, approvals, sign-offs and meetings makes it hard to reach decisions, let alone carry them out. These difficulties were illustrated clearly in IBM's efforts to develop desktop computers. The only way they were successful was to appoint a small group of people to develop the product and then remove them from the company's normal reporting systems. The result was the extraordinarily successful IBM personal computer.

Centralized decision making worked when managers knew the jobs they supervised and organizations had relatively few managers. With the changing nature of work and the need to respond to continuously changing customer preferences, centralized decision-making systems are a hindrance.

High volume rigid systems

In the post-World War II period, our organizations were remarkable for their ability to produce extraordinarily large numbers of products. A growing population absorbed everything produced and even demanded more. The difficulty now is that we have gone too far. We have over 15,000 banks in the United States and most observers agree this is more than we need.[88] Real estate agents will readily tell you that we have more real estate agents than necessary, and, in some instances, these superfluous agents are unprofessional or otherwise incapable of carrying out their responsibilities.[89]

The belief that we can meet the needs of people we serve by getting bigger and doing more is slowly giving way to the idea that we have to continuously introduce new products and services that meet increasingly individualized personal needs.

Specialization

At the World's Fair in 1876, Queen Victoria's consort, Prince Albert, gave a speech extolling the glories of specialization.[90] Specialization is a useful idea when manufacturing systems are simple, but it adds to our problems when systems are complex.

In larger, more complex organizations, specialization makes it hard for people in one part of highly compartmentalized systems to see the meaning of what they do. Work becomes meaningless and counter-productive. A Citicorp loan officer who specialized in making loans to the Third World during the 1980s was a significant contributor to the company's half-billion dollar loss in 1992. If he or she had seen the broader picture and hadn't been quite so efficient, Citicorp would have suffered fewer losses.

■

Managing information

Existing arrangements in large organizations also make it difficult to manage information. It takes too much time to move information up, down and across the traditional hierarchy, in part because the number of people involved virtually ensures that the information will be garbled, distorted or filtered. The result is that organizations have difficulty dealing with reality. In his book, *The Presidency In Flux,* George Reedy made the point that when things were going well there was a stampede to the President's office to report good news. When there was bad news, everybody was out of town.[91] In the same vein, W. Thomas Stevens, chief executive of the Manville Corporation, discusses what he describes as CEO's disease — the difficulties CEOs have in identifying, let alone coming to grips, with reality.[92] As another example, in a memo inadvertently released by a staff member, IBM's former chairman John Akers said he was "sick of being told by the staff that things were wonderful and by customers that deliveries were late."[93] Existing arrangements make it hard, if not impossible, to get the right information to the right person at the right time.

Each of these issues is exacerbated by size, but the question has more to do with how we arrange ourselves to manage information rather than how big we are. Simply changing the size of an organization won't solve anything.

■ REQUIREMENTS FOR SUCCESS

"It ain't nuclear physics."
— *Anonymous*

The requirements for organizational success are clear. Organizations need to develop products and services people will buy, ensure quality and achieve financial soundness.

> *"The bigger we get, the smaller I want our employees to think and act."*
> —Herb Kelleher, CEO
> Southwest Airlines

Managing change

In the relatively stable world of our past, success came from doing more of what we were doing. During times of turbulence, the reverse is true. Our challenge is to continuously develop new products and services, as well as simpler and more effective ways to accomplish what we need to. We do not need layers of management or people whose only role is to move information.

Quality

It used to be that organizations could pretty much sell what they produced: the quality of a given product or service was by and large determined by the producer rather than the user. Quality is discussed in the next chapter, so for the moment we need only note that there is growing agreement that it means:

- meeting customer expectations; and
- doing "the appropriate thing correctly the first time."

We can no longer afford products or services that are just "good enough," nor can we tolerate redundant or wasteful work. Increasing complexity may be an asset when we are trying to justify the need for bigger budgets and more staff, but it makes meeting customer needs difficult. Adding one staff person in a department may be important, but when 10 people reach that decision the cost goes into hundreds of thousands of dollars. Similarly, adding just one form doesn't hurt until 10 people do it and the forms they create contradict each other or create redundant work.

Demands for quality will continue to rise and the inevitable result will be that successful organizations will develop simpler systems that make it easier to meet people's needs with fewer staff.

Financial soundness

Perhaps no organizational issue causes as much frustration as an organization's budget process. Managers with individual responsibilities frequently believe they should reinvest earnings in their own operations. In successful organizations capital questions are dealt with by senior management because they are expected to have the perspective necessary to decide whether to invest in existing businesses or new opportunities. This approach makes it possible to hold managers accountable for performance without meddling in how the organization operates.

When there are difficulties with financial performance, too many organizations move the responsibility for budgeting further up the line or add additional approval steps to control people at lower levels. Rather than solving the problem, these approaches invariably slow the system, increase costs and add to complexity. The alternative is to better train managers to handle financial issues and then to replace those who are unable to carry out their responsibilities.

Another reason bigger is no longer better is that it is too expensive. We can no longer afford the layers of management and staff that we had in the industrial society. During that period we solved problems by throwing money or people at them. Now we need to solve them by redesigning the way we work to accomplish what we need to with fewer resources.

Human nature is such that when each of us is hired, our behavior follows a predictable pattern. First, we schedule meetings with our boss to be sure he/she knows that our work is important. Second, we write memos and take other people's time in meetings to be sure they know we've talked to the boss and what we are doing is important. (The average memo takes 45 minutes to write and costs $65,[94] not to mention the costs related to what other people do with it.) Third, we generate sufficient activity, constructive or otherwise, that we inevitably talk to our boss in six months or a year about adding more staff. The pattern isn't malicious, but it is predictable. The way to control it is to stop hiring.

Financial soundness requires using fewer, more effective people. Two questions to ask before hiring are: 1) can he or she make a contribution to customer service, and 2) can he or she help build for the future? If the potential employee can't, we don't need them.

One lesson of the 1980s was that organizations with lower overhead costs were more successful than those with large corporate costs. Wal-Mart surpassed Sears as the nation's largest retailer primarily because its overhead costs were 5 percent lower.

In many cases, organizational budgeting processes are time consuming, excessively complex and unproductive. Simplifying management systems so that managers have information on the company's overall goals, direction and expectations reduces the amount of time necessary to complete what should be a productive rather than frustrating ritual.

It is unlikely that we will be able to produce quality products and services or manage change using traditional systems. The question isn't whether we should centralize or decentralize, but how we can rearrange ourselves to achieve our goals.

■ ALTERNATIVE ARRANGEMENTS

"There will always be a better way."
— *Anonymous*

Most of us grew up in a period in which the traditional hierarchy was the standard organizational form. This organizational model enabled us to accomplish work that had previously been beyond our capabilities. However, most of us are so familiar with the hierarchy that we tend not to think of other arrangements that may be better. The hierarchy has such a strong hold on our minds that it's hard to look beyond it. In reality, hierarchies are just one among a number of organizational possibilities and over the coming decade, we will continue to experiment and work with alternatives.

The orchestra as an organizational model

Peter Drucker has talked about the idea of the orchestra as an organizational model.[95] His analogy is useful because an orchestra has characteristics that would be helpful in any organization. First, every member knows the score as well as his or her own part. Second, orchestras have no hierarchies. The first violinist plays the violin as well as coordinating the work of the rest of the violinists. Third, an orchestra always practices. Some of these practices are public performances, but the focus is on continuous improvement. Fourth, an orchestra is an interdependent organization — the whole depends on its parts. Mistakes reflect on the entire orchestra rather than an individual musician. The importance of working together is illustrated in the fact that even in truly great orchestras, we rarely know the names of individual musicians. Finally, the conductor rarely plays an instrument. Conductors, as Drucker points out, usually can't do the work they supervise. The responsibility of the conductor is to determine the works to be played, how they will be arranged and to help each musician accomplish what needs to be done to ensure the success of the whole.

The diamond

In the diamond organization the customer is at the center. At the top, senior management teams develop rules that focus on the overall work of the organization. The 3M Corporation, for example, has the goal to earn 25 percent of its net income from ideas that are less than five years old.[96] In the bottom half of the diamond, people are encouraged to work together to find ways to accomplish goals. At 3M the process is controlled by an insistence that all staff follow the 3M "approach to quality." In a diamond organization, the goals, rules and process are specified at the top, while individual decisions are the responsibility of people throughout the company. Management's responsibility is to ensure that the company's goals are met and to maintain the integrity of the process.

Customer-driven organizations

Customer-driven organizations are arranged to meet the needs of people they serve rather than the people who run them. The most important staff members are direct service providers — people who do work for customers. Managers support their efforts and the responsibility of leadership is to simplify systems to enable service providers to do their jobs well.

The customer-driven organization accomplishes its work through teams made up of people from different departments. Department boundaries blur and staff members work collaboratively to satisfy customers. In traditional hierarchical arrangements — whether they are centralized or decentralized — customers go from department to department. However, since customers don't segment their concerns by company departments, in the customer-driven organization people from different departments are organized to meet the needs of the customer.

Training is provided across traditional departmental boundaries so the organization can bring people together to learn what the organization does and how they can work together to support the people they serve. Individuals throughout the organization are cross-trained so they can respond flexibly to the needs of the customer. The emphasis is on speed and collaboration.

The doughnut

The doughnut may be the oddest of the alternative organizational arrangements. In the doughnut, the organization is arranged with customers and information at its core — the hole of the doughnut. Personnel are organized around customers and information. Boundaries are blurred or non-existent. Every employee and every team has access to information; whether the information is related to financial systems, market preferences, production schedules or any other aspect of the operation. These teams respond to individual customers or markets to meet their needs. The doughnut is the most common form of organization for start-up businesses. In the beginning, there are no management layers or titles. Personnel anticipate the need to share information and performance.

The common theme through each of these organizational possibilities is that questions about centralization or decentralization are irrelevant. What is important is how we arrange ourselves to accomplish what needs to be done.

■ BETTER WAYS OF DOING THINGS

> "If you're a hammer in life, everything looks like a nail."
>
> — *Anonymous*

The reality of change is making it easier to think about organizations differently. There is a growing emphasis on thinking about how we arrange work we need to do and the result is better discussions that usually focus on functions and how they are handled instead of departments and how they are structured.

Policy and operations

In successful organizations senior executives deal with policy and managers run operations. Senior management's attention is on corporate issues such as organizational values, strategic direction and other factors critical for continuing success. Leaders continuously involve employees in discussions about the organization's values, purpose and direction so that everyone knows what is expected. In these organizations senior management's responsibility is to clarify and simplify policy while encouraging people throughout the organization to use their talents to meet customer needs and make changes necessary to manage the future.

One example of this approach is Bank One's "uncommon partnership." Bank One's policy is to centralize paper and decentralize people. Bank One's reporting and information systems enable managers throughout the organization to do their jobs by reducing the need for senior managers to make decisions about individual transactions. This approach enables each of Bank One's several hundred branches to respond to the needs of individuals and businesses in the communities they serve without going up the line to get approvals for what they need to do.

Several years ago, Charles "Mike" Harper, former chief executive of ConAgra, spoke to beef growers in Colorado. Following his presentation, Colorado ranchers asked Harper numerous questions about ConAgra's operations and how he saw the future. As individual issues were raised, Harper's response was almost always to say that he "didn't know very much about it." He would then ask the ConAgra executive who had actually done the work to answer the question. Harper resisted the temptation to become involved in operating decisions and delegated both the credit and the responsibility for ConAgra's achievements to the people who actually did the work.

This focus on clarifying policy and operating responsibilities frees up people to contribute to discussions about policy and, more importantly, gives them the responsibility and authority to do what needs to be done. Organizations in which senior staff constantly intervene in daily operations are generally organizations unable to clarify the difference between policy and operations. They are muddled about their own future and how they run their business. Distinguishing between policy and operations enables everyone in an organization to understand its overall values and direction while simultaneously freeing them to do their jobs effectively.

Information and computers

The challenge in managing information systems effectively is the paradox inherent in simultaneously trying to take advantage of large system capabilities while making information widely available throughout the organization.

The objective for organizations isn't to build bigger computer capabilities, but to design information systems that meet people's needs. Integrating both large and small systems enables us to use personal computers to access almost any information required. Given the increasingly rapid developments in computer technology the question of whether we centralize or decentralize computer systems is obsolete. The primary issue is how we design computers to ensure that people have the information they need to do their jobs.

Marketing and sales

As customer preferences change and markets become increasingly distinct, successful organizations have developed their overall marketing approach and delegated the responsibility for sales and service to people closest to the customer. The Home Depot discount hardware stores are a good example. The corporate responsibility is to position the company in the market. Individual managers make decisions about inventory levels, products they sell and how they meet customer needs.

The growth of franchise systems in real estate and automotive parts is another example. In franchise arrangements, certain functions are dealt with by senior management, while others are managed by franchise holders. ReMax, one of the nation's largest real estate companies, provides marketing support to its agents, who in turn have the responsibility to work with clients.

We have become so familiar with the issues related to scale that it's difficult to accept the idea that we need to think about things differently. Abraham Lincoln was once asked how long a person's legs should be and his answer was, "long enough to reach the ground." It is clear we will have to devote more attention to clarifying what we are trying to accomplish and then decide how we can do it. In most cases, this approach will lead to significant changes in how we structure and operate our organizations.

AN OBSESSION WITH QUALITY

CHAPTER FIVE

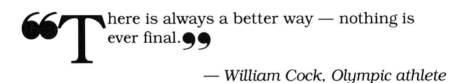

"There is always a better way — nothing is ever final.**"**

— William Cock, Olympic athlete

Inside...

- Understanding quality

- The costs of poor quality

- Facing reality

- Making progress

- Quality improvement principles

■ AN OBSESSION WITH QUALITY

"What was top quality seven years ago is now junk.[97]
— *Harold DeNeal, retired steel worker*

One reality of the 1990s is that we can no longer afford shoddy products. At the zenith of the industrial society, waste didn't much matter. Increasing real incomes and a growing population masked the costs of inefficiency and poor products. Most of us accepted the idea that the way things were was what we should expect. Mystery writer John D. McDonald captured the spirit of those times in his 1953 book, *Cancel All Our Vows.* McDonald's central character thinks about his car and muses, "the car would be two years old in October with only 31,000 miles. Maybe it would be simpler just to get a new one."[98]

In the 1950s and 1960s most businesses believed that while some products would be returned, they were doing as well as they could — or should. In 1977, an employee at the Oryx Corporation figured out a new way to pay federal royalties and save the company about $35,000 a month. Asked why he hadn't suggested the idea earlier, he responded, "Before, nobody cared."[99] In 1989, IBM paid $4.4 billion in warranty costs. This meant IBM spent money on $4.4 billion worth of mistakes. This figure doesn't count the costs of paperwork and time to pay the warranties. Waste such as IBM's always has two costs: the cost of the waste itself and the opportunities missed because we had to pay for that waste. If their products had been better made, IBM could have spent that same $4.4 billion for new product development, customer service, training, salary increases or shareholder dividends.

Times are changing. Over the coming years successful organizations will become obsessed with "quality" — the idea that we can always find a better way. They will know they can no longer afford the waste associated with weak systems and poor quality. Most important, they will understand that we must perform well all the time. They will strive not just to be good enough, but to be as good as they can possibly be.

∎ Understanding Quality

> "A change is ordered in the way we conduct our business."
> — *Robert C. Hanna, president/CEO Imperial Holly Corp.*[100]

One promising development has been the growing consensus on what quality actually means. This emerging consensus is based on two points. First, we should meet customer expectations, and second, we should "do the appropriate thing correctly the first time." Financial statements from banks, insurance companies and hospitals should be accurate. Toasters, ovens and VCRs should work without having to be replaced. In the simplest terms, whether we follow W. Edwards Deming and call it "conforming to customer expectations,"[101] or Joseph Juran and focus on producing products that are "fit for use,"[102] we should meet the needs of the people we serve.

The 180 steps in the real estate closing process make it hard to manage, and as anyone who has bought a home knows, the process is time consuming and maddening. The benefits of meeting customer needs correctly the first time are significant. We can, as Deming argues, retain the customers we have, attract new customers and reduce the costs of meeting their needs.[103]

To act on these two points, we need to work differently. First, we need to simplify everything we do. We have to eliminate unnecessary work and paper because both are expensive and frustrating. Most systems we have developed are unneccessarily complex and make it difficult to do our jobs effectively. The more steps there are in a process, the more likely we are to make mistakes.

We also need to develop much more disciplined systems to control what we do. Many of us tend to believe that discipline inhibits creativity when in fact it makes creativity possible. If systems and their rules are explicit, clear and well known, then we are free to do our job. It is when rules are unclear and systems are undisciplined that we have to spend time figuring out what's going on, rather than creatively improving what we do. There are many positive examples. One is the earlier example of 3M Corporation changing its refund policies so sales representatives make decisions about customer refunds — eliminating 52 steps in the process. This led to more satisfied customers and saved 3M approximately $15 million per year.[104]

We have to reorganize work around the concept of continuous change rather than the idea of stability. One of the primary themes of quality efforts is that there is always room for improvement. Quality is a journey, not a trip. A second theme is that people are capable, but often the systems we use are weak. We have the opportunity to support people while we continuously redesign the way we work.

Improving quality means that we have to pay attention to the soft side of the organization. Issues such as shared goals, mutual respect and trust become prerequisites that enable people to focus on meeting the needs of those they serve rather than their own personal needs or those of their departments. We also need to learn to love critics because, as mentioned earlier, they represent the easiest and quickest way to identify problems.

■ THE COSTS OF POOR QUALITY

"Funny thing, civilization: it promises so much and what it delivers is mass production of shoddy merchandise and shoddy people."
— *Stuart Kaminsky*
Murder on the Yellow Brick Road[105]

Understanding what happens when we don't "do the appropriate thing correctly the first time" makes it easier to see why quality is so important. Jeff Dewar, of the quality consulting firm QCI International, developed a list of what the world would look like if we were able to do our jobs correctly 99.9 percent of the time. Even then, we would still have:

- one hour of unsafe drinking water every month;
- two unsafe plane landings at Chicago's O'Hare International Airport every day;
- 16,000 pieces of mail lost by the U.S. Post Office every hour;
- 20,000 incorrect drug prescriptions each year;
- 500 incorrect surgical operations each week;
- 50 newborn babies dropped at birth by doctors every day; and
- 22,000 checks deducted from the wrong bank account every hour.[106]

Each of us can assess the quality of what we do by applying Dewar's formula to our own organizations. Remember, Dewar was talking about a world in which we did the appropriate thing correctly 99.9 percent of the time — a standard we clearly haven't reached. We have become so complacent regarding performance that we are all too frequently insensitive to the waste and breakdowns we observe every day. Examples include security guards at airports, the growing cost of police departments and prisons, the cost of accidents in the home and on the job, the costs of cleaning up toxic waste, and costs associated with returning or repairing defective products.

The costs of poor quality always show up in three ways: lost customers, wasted time and wasted money. A clear example of how to lose customers involves the Old National Bank in Spokane, Wash., and a customer named John Barrier. On one of his visits to the bank, Barrier asked a teller to validate his parking ticket. She told him she could not and referred him to a manager. Barrier says the manager looked at him like he had "crawled out from under a rock" and declined to stamp his 35 cent parking ticket. The result was that Barrier moved his account, which turned out to be more than $1 million. When it was all over, Barrier observed that, "If you have a hundred dollars in the bank or a million dollars, I think they owe you the courtesy of stamping your parking ticket."[107]

Waste goes up when we don't understand the true costs of "business as usual." Most of the managers we have worked with estimate that they could cut paperwork by 25 to 40 percent and argue that about the same percentage of the meet-

> *The problem in the United States isn't that we have too many meetings, but that we have the same meeting over and over again.*

ings they attend are equally wasteful. The problem in the United States isn't that we have too many meetings, but that we have the same meeting over and over again. We run meetings as if they were all the same and as a result, usually end up repeating similar discussions about the same issues.

The three reasons people in organizations come together are to learn, to share information and to make decisions. We usually run meetings as if they were all decision meetings. The result is that we deny ourselves the opportunity and freedom to explore possibilities in learning sessions or to share information without feeling we have to make a decision.

A third area of waste is the cost of complexity and the common need to redo work we have already done. Jack Welch, chairman of General Electric, argues that "the demand for simplicity applies to every one of us. To an engineer, it means clean, functional designs with fewer parts. For manufacturers, it means judging a process not by how sophisticated it is, but how understandable it is to those who must make it work."[108] Complex systems are inherently fragile and lead to mistakes because they are hard to understand and operate. They also take more people to manage. An example: Until the early 1990s, General Motors made cars on 21 different platforms and the costs associated with training, tooling, parts and design were all higher than they would have been if GM used fewer platforms. In contrast, Southwest Airlines flies only Boeing 737 airplanes. The result is a sharp reduction in the costs of training, parts, repairs and errors since people have to master only one system.

In addition to these costs, Harvard business school professor Rosabeth Moss-Kanter has identified the additional, intangible costs of ineffective systems. Kanter cites the costs of confusion and not knowing what we're doing; the cost of misinformation, which results in wasted energy or not doing what needs to be done; the "emotional leakage" that occurs when people don't care about what they're doing; the loss of energy because people are uninterested or unable to do what needs to be done; and the breakdowns that occur when we do not care about or assume responsibility for the quality of what we do.[109]

These costs are all real. The challenge lies in accepting the idea that the world is changed and, while we could afford these costs in the 1950s, we can't afford them today.

■ FACING REALITY

"The devil made me do it."
— *Comedian Flip Wilson*

While there is a growing consensus concerning the importance of quality, there are at the same time powerful distractions. We discuss these distractions as if they were the source of our difficulties and in doing so miss the point that they are challenges to be managed, not reasons for poor performance.

Foreign trade problems

One distraction is the argument that United States companies trade with nations who compete unfairly. The foreign trade argument — particularly frustration with Japan — misses the point for two reasons. First, our largest trading partners are Canada, Mexico and Japan, in that order. Japan may be the most visible, but it is not the largest. Further, focusing on the difficulties inherent in foreign trade saps energy and attention that should go to improving our own products and services. Second, the reality is that we now live and will continue to live in a global economy. Competitive pressures will increase, not decrease which means that our first priority has to be to produce high-quality and consumer-oriented products and services. Then, we can and should spend time on trade arrangements and the structure of the global economy. What we think of as fair trade won't help if the quality of what we make won't stand up in the emerging global marketplace.

Value of the dollar

A second argument is that the value of the dollar makes it hard for domestic companies to compete globally. While the value of the dollar obviously affects the attractiveness of American goods and services, this argument belies the reality that there are customers willing to pay for high-quality products and services. In 1989, Honda was the best selling automobile in the United States. While you could argue that this was partly because of the value of the dollar, it was also clear that customers felt Honda made better cars. Fluctuations in the dollar do not explain the fact that increasing numbers of Americans purchase foreign cars and other foreign products. Even when prices are comparable, Americans often buy foreign products because they believe these products provide better value.

Unions

Many managers argue that we would be better off without unions. In the 1920s and 1930s, unions were an important mechanism to secure safe working conditions and fair wages for millions of Americans. Focusing on union activity in the 1990s is another good example of letting ourselves get caught up in the whirlwind rather than focusing on more important issues. Unions exist for the same reason they always have: Employees unionize because they feel they are being treated unfairly. To argue that unions should be eliminated is to miss the point. Each of us is responsible for ensuring that people are treated fairly and know the value of the work they do.

In addition, there are numerous concerns about the relationships between unions and companies. All of them are more constructively addressed when they are seen as issues to be managed rather than explanations for poor performance.

Government regulations

Government regulation is another popular whipping boy for difficulties in the American economy. The amount of red tape and paperwork, the complexity of laws and regulations and a host of other sins, both real and imagined, are all laid at the door of state and federal governments to explain why we can't compete. This argument overlooks the point that business people in Canada, Japan and other countries share many of the same regulatory burdens. The reality is that government regulation is part of every society, not a condition peculiar to the United States.

In most cases, governments regulate business activity for one of two reasons. First, organizations resist emerging issues rather than working to resolve them. The efforts of car makers and steel producers to weaken or avoid environmental legislation is one example. Second, governments invariably intervene when professionals are unwilling to manage the ethics and behavior of their colleagues. E.F. Hutton would not have had to deal with regulations, lawsuits or the courts if the company had not defrauded its banks.[110] Some regulations are indeed spurious, but most are a result of breakdowns in business practices. Once we focus on doing what we should do for the people we serve, the result will be decreased regulation and lower cost of doing business.

Customers

The final argument is perhaps the most extreme. Some managers and employees actually argue that the problem is their customers. Customers are the reason we are able to work, not an insurmountable problem.

There are parts of each of these arguments that are true. There are difficulties in trading agreements with nations around the world. There are problems with the fluctuating value of the dollar, and there are real difficulties because of governmental regulation. But our emphasis on these problems distracts us from accomplishing what we need to do. We have to focus on quality, both because we can manage it and because resolving these other issues won't matter if we can't produce goods and services customers will buy.

■ MAKING PROGRESS

"The relentless pursuit of excellence."
— *Advertisement for Lexus Cars*

Ivan Welborn, a vice president of Findley Adhesives Inc., Milwaukee, was so interested in quality that he worked out examples of what the cost of poor quality might be at each step in any given process. Figure 2, on the following page, summarizes his work.

The chart illustrates that making an error that affects a customer has significant ramifications. The costs are significant because, as discussed in Chapter Three, every dissatisfied customer will tell at least one other person and 13 percent will tell approximately 20 friends.[111] Paradoxically, if we focus on quality, as opposed to making money, net income will go up. Welborn also developed a chart (Figure 3, page 81) to show the effects of two strategies; one focused on increased income and the second focused on improving quality.

Many companies have begun to accept the idea that we have to improve quality, in some instances, because of problems in their businesses. Jack Telnack, vice president for design at the Ford Motor Company, says that at Ford, "We had the luxury of adversity" — things were done so badly at Ford they had no choice but to rethink how they ran the business.[112] Whether improvements in quality are the result of "luxury of adversity" or

Figure 2
The cost of quality
or
the cost of errors, defects and defect prevention

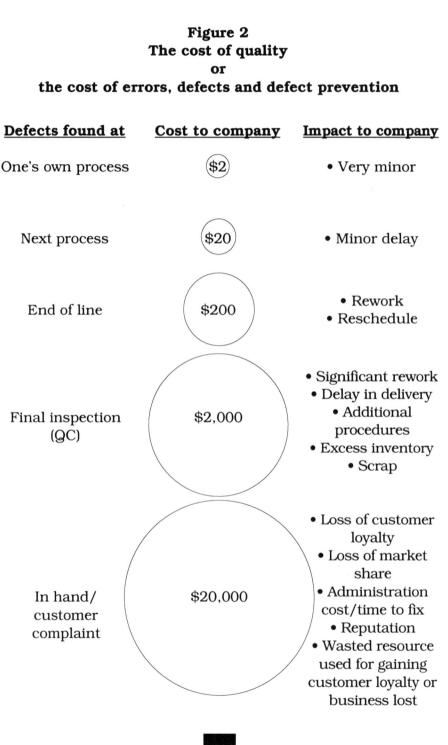

Defects found at	Cost to company	Impact to company
One's own process	$2	• Very minor
Next process	$20	• Minor delay
End of line	$200	• Rework • Reschedule
Final inspection (QC)	$2,000	• Significant rework • Delay in delivery • Additional procedures • Excess inventory • Scrap
In hand/ customer complaint	$20,000	• Loss of customer loyalty • Loss of market share • Administration cost/time to fix • Reputation • Wasted resource used for gaining customer loyalty or business lost

---

Figure 3
Selling more vs. improved quality

OPTION A: *Sell more to double profit*

	Year 1	**Year 2**
Sales	$100,000,000	$200,000,000
Resources invested	80,000,000	160,000,000
Cost of quality	15,000,000	30,000,000
Profit:	5,000,000	10,000,000

OPTION B: *Improve quality to double profit*

	Year 1	**Year 2**
Sales	$100,000,000	$100,000,000
Resources invested	80,000,000	80,000,000
Cost of quality	15,000,000	10,000,000
Profit:	5,000,000	10,000,000

the willingness of strong organizations, such as the 3M Corporation, to examine what they do and how they do it, there are growing numbers of examples of what is possible. These examples fall into two broad categories:

- improving the design of products and services; and
- improving systems.

Design

There are numerous examples of design improvements. The Ford Taurus is one of the most visible and dramatic. By involving engineers, designers, marketing people and manufacturing staff in the design, planning and building of the Taurus, Ford produced an automobile that met or exceeded consumer expectations. Not surprisingly, Ford's design ideas have been emulated by most other car makers. Similarly, Black & Decker introduced cordless tools that make it possible to work in a tool shop, the yard or the house without constantly looking for electrical outlets. IBM has reduced the number of parts in its ProPrinter by 65 percent, thereby reducing assembly time and defects.[113] Xerox also reduced the number of moving parts in its copiers which reduced down time and the likelihood of failure. Other examples of design improvements include simple things such as the snap-lid for a box of Tide. People who do the family laundry appreciate a box designed to reduce spillage. Drano, the liquid drain cleaner, now comes in containers with see-through strips so customers can see how much is left in the bottle.

Companies that have been able to improve design have usually involved designers, manufacturers, marketing and research and development staff in the design of their products and services. The result is a richer, shared understanding of how the customer actually uses the product, as well as how it can be more simply manufactured. Consistent with the idea of an information society, the emphasis is on substituting intelligence for mass. It is easier and significantly less expensive to think through how a product or service will meet a customer's needs rather than making subsequent adjustments in the manufacturing process or marketing systems.

Systems

There are increasingly numerous examples of companies improving the systems and procedures they use to accomplish work. Corning reduced defects in its television panels from 4 percent to .03 percent. At a 4 percent defect rate, Corning was producing products they couldn't sell. Reducing the defect rate improved output and plant capacity expanded 40 percent. Another example is Shearson Lehman's reduction of bond redemption time by 50 percent and the improved accuracy of the process from 80 percent to approximately 90 percent. Whistler, the company that produces "Fuzz Buster" car radar systems, increased the number of products that were "fit for use" from 75 percent to 99 percent and ITT reduced defects by 50 percent with an estimated savings of $60 million.[114]

In each of the cases the emphasis on redesigning systems is focused on making them simpler. Simpler systems with fewer parts and fewer steps are easier for people to understand and manage. During the industrial period when we focused on the organization, each of us had an interest in adding complexity to the systems of which we were a part. Complexity provided a rationale for the importance of our jobs and an ongoing reason to hire additional people.

> *Simpler systems with fewer parts and fewer steps are easier for people to understand and manage.*

■ QUALITY IMPROVEMENT PRINCIPLES

"The search for perfection is the only perfection there is."
— *William Schuman*[115]
Juilliard School

While we are still learning what it takes to improve quality, there is growing agreement on principles that should guide our efforts.

Quality can always get better

Improving quality requires a commitment to the idea that we can always get better. In the world of continuous improvement there is no such thing as a steady state. This commitment means that every quality effort is based on standards with two characteristics: first, standards are high; and second, they continue to rise. Perry Pascarella, vice president of *Industry Week* magazine, writes, "A 7 percent error rate may sound good ... but express that as 70,000 in a million and you're asking the customer to overlook 70,000 shortcomings."[116] The point is that we always have to get better.

Quality is everybody's business

If we want quality to improve, everyone must help. In the industrial society we were interested in people's physical capabilities. Bosses would do the thinking and employees would do the work. This view has changed. It is increasingly important to accept that every person at every level of the organization knows something that can lead to improvements. Successful managers focus on the intellectual, emotional and physical capabilities of their staffs so that each has the interest, commitment and skills to contribute to improving quality.

Data matters

Appropriate information is essential for organizations seeking to improve quality. Running organizations on the basis of intuition, what we have always done or how we think the organization works, frequently is inadequate. We have to be clear about what is important to measure and understand that the need for measurements will change as the organization changes. If we become captives of existing data, we lose our ability to design more effective ways to accomplish what is required.

Departments must work together

Whether we focus on individuals, departments, organizations or nations, improving quality is a function of how closely different groups work together. Our commitment to specialization led us to create industrial organizations in which departments were rigidly separate — finance was separate from manufacturing, which was separate from sales, which was separate from research. At a broader level, we organized industries around specialized products and services, and on a national level, we drew clear boundaries between the public and the private sectors. Focusing on quality means we need to organize around the work to be done rather than the skills or interests of people who do the work. The focus has to be on the process rather than the department. Improvements in quality will be the result of managing work across professional or organizational boundaries and the biggest gains will come from collaborative efforts across departments within an organization, across organizations themselves and, more broadly, between public, private and "third sector" organizations.

Patience is essential

Improvements in quality don't just happen; they are the result of deliberate, focused, consistent and sustained effort. It takes time to build an understanding and acceptance of the idea that quality can be improved. This includes time to build the trust and relationships essential to help people work together effectively. Quality requires a commitment, and building commitment takes time.

Next steps

Successful efforts to improve quality all have common characteristics.

First, the leaders of successful organizations or departments are personally committed to improving quality. Their commitment is reflected in their willingness to attend training sessions to acquire the skills and understanding necessary to provide direction for the overall effort.

Second, staff at all levels of the organization have the opportunity to be trained in quality — what it means and what they can do to improve what they do. Staff have the opportunity to acquire skills in areas such as statistics, process management and facilitation skills to help them do what needs to be done.

Third, organizations are willing to redesign their information and management systems to focus on what matters and support people throughout the organization. The emphasis is on getting the right information to the right people at the right time.

Quality is not a magic bullet but it is, and will continue to be, an essential component of changes we need to make.

COLLABORATION:

LEARNING TO WORK TOGETHER

CHAPTER SIX

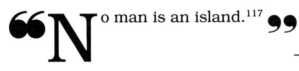

"No man is an island.[117]**"**

— Rev. John Donne

Inside...

- Collaborative efforts and what they do

- Running the organization more effectively

- Collaboration and competition

- Challenges and opportunities

- Building collaborative relationships

■ COLLABORATION: LEARNING TO WORK TOGETHER

"We will either work together or hang separately."
— *Anonymous*

For most of the industrial period we believed in specialization and prided ourselves on being independent. Our commitments to specialization and independence were organizing ideas in how we structured our families, our jobs and our organizations. Expectations for mothers and fathers emphasized their individual roles in raising children rather than their shared responsibilities. Over time job descriptions became increasingly distinct and individually defined. Our organizations became collections of independent units increasingly focused on their own work and well being rather than the organization as a whole or the people they served.

One part of the shift in how we view the world has been a reassessment of our views concerning the value of specialization and independence. We have begun to accept the idea that in most cases we can accomplish more by working together than we can by working alone. We have developed a variety of words to describe these efforts — collaboration, networking, strategic alliances, linking-up and partnering are just a few — but, regardless of the words we use, the theme is consistent.

- We are changing how we think about the responsibilities of men and women as parents. There is a greater emphasis on sharing the responsibilities for raising children and running a home — especially when both parents work.
- Organizations working to improve quality and meet customer expectations invariably focus on the need for people with different responsibilities to work with each other more closely.

- Economic development efforts in communities across the country focus on the need for business people, educators, health executives and public officials to work together on common community goals.
- Increasingly national governments work on issues related to economic prosperity and, at the other extreme, military action in concert with other nations rather than unilaterally.

There are two ideas which underlie every successful collaborative effort. The first is a commitment to a goal that is more valued than the needs of an individual, a single department or a single organization. Whether raising a child, serving a customer or building a community, participants are able to look beyond their own narrow parochial interests. Second, there is a recognition that the goal cannot be achieved alone. While we are often still awkward in building collaborative relationships, we are gradually learning more about how to make them work.

■ COLLABORATIVE EFFORTS AND WHAT THEY DO

> "The 1990s will be known as the decade of linkages."
> — *Harold "Bud" Hodgkinson*[118]

Collaborative efforts are important for two reasons: they enable us to learn more than we would otherwise and they help us accomplish work we couldn't do by ourselves.

Learning together

During periods of stability we can usually rely on our own experience to make decisions, but during periods of change we need to learn from others who may have developed different approaches to issues we face. When efforts to help people learn collaboratively are effective, it is usually because they have been structured along one of two dimensions.

The first is the development of collaborative learning arrangements to help people learn more about their own profession or industry. Associations, and in some cases consulting firms, have played a major role in meeting this need by developing certification programs and providing continuing professional education.

Associations and consulting firms have also undertaken collaborative research work to help their members or clients. The Medical Group Management Association (MGMA) and The National Association of Realtors (NAR), for example, both publish "cost of doing business" surveys[119] that analyze the effectiveness of members' business practices. The Food Management Institute (FMI) analyzes patterns and trends in the food business. Their work on the products sold in different kinds of stores such as supermarkets, hyper markets and boutiques; help members plan and manage their individual businesses more effectively. Price Waterhouse develops similar information to assist law firms, and J.D. Powers, the marketing research firm, monitors customer preferences in the automotive industry. In addition, a growing number of associations develop information on issues such as environmental assessment and changes in the social, economic and political fabric of the United States, while others provide analyses of legislative or regulatory issues that could affect their members.

These collaborative efforts have significant benefits. First, they enable members to acquire information that might otherwise be unavailable. Competitors are often unwilling or, in some cases, unable to share information directly. Using third-party mechanisms such as associations or consulting firms enables them to provide information anonymously and gain the benefits of learning about the effectiveness of various practices in their own industry. Second, the cost of such work is shared by participants and, as a result, is much less expensive than it would be if individual firms undertook the work alone.

On a second dimension, some learning activities are organized around the principle that, during turbulent times, truly valuable learning comes from sharing ideas with people outside

■

... during turbulent times, truly valuable learning comes from sharing ideas with people outside our own field.

our own field. Bankers can learn about marketing and sales from retailers. Social service professionals can usually learn more about quality and managing work flow from manufacturers than they can from colleagues in their own field. People who follow the traditions in any given field frequently learn more than they otherwise would by working with outsiders who have addressed similar issues from a different perspective. These perspectives may come from clients, suppliers or people in totally different industries.

Some efforts are organized around issues common to people in totally different businesses. The Executive Committee (TEC) in Milwaukee is a good example. Each TEC group has approximately a dozen chief executives who are supported by a staff person called a TEC chairperson. This person works with members to identify issues they can productively address. Each meeting is divided into two parts. In the first, TEC members work with an outside resource person while the second half of each session provides time for members to work on issues that affect their own businesses. In effect, members of TEC groups serve as informal advisors for each other. TEC forums provide an opportunity for CEOs to candidly discuss issues with peers who have dealt with similar issues from different perspectives. Another example of this same approach is the American Society of Association Executives (ASAE). While ASAE members may work in different fields, the Association helps them address issues common to association management. There are similar examples in the fields of social service, communications and financial services.

One of the paradoxes of turbulent times is that we need specialists who are better generalists, and generalists who are better specialists. No successful manager can operate effectively without, for example, an understanding of the impact of computers on his or her business. Conversely, computer technical staff cannot be truly effective without understanding their role in the organization and how they contribute to its success. Peter Drucker has pointed out that managers who want to be successful in the 1990s will have to take responsibility for their own learning and development[120] and one method to accomplish this is to seek out learning opportunities that cross traditional boundaries.

Doing work

Collaborative efforts to accomplish work are increasingly common both within and among organizations. They are successful when people have clear goals; they fail when participants are unwilling or unable to subordinate their individual interests to achieve these broader goals. One striking characteristic of collaborative efforts is the range of activities they embrace.

Running the organization more effectively

Organizations are finding they can frequently achieve their individual goals by working with others to accomplish what they need to do rather than by trying to do it alone.

Federal and state land management agencies have found they can meet their individual missions and manage public lands more effectively by trading land parcels or managing them collaboratively rather than independently.

Colgate Palmolive restructured its marketing arrangements because it believed it could develop more effective advertising by working closely with a limited number of advertising agencies rather than continuing traditional industry arrangements. Colgate fired its 13 advertising agencies and instead formed partnerships with just two. Colgate worked with the two agencies to help them set up shop wherever Colgate did business. The relationship was structured so the two firms could focus on Colgate's long-term success rather than worrying about short-term contracts.[122] IBM

> *"Teamwork ... every time we find success in this organization, it ultimately boils down to that important ingredient."*
> — Scott Jones [121]
> Goodhue County Financial Corp.

has hundreds of similar joint ventures all formed to meet the needs of customers or improve the company's product development capabilities.[123]

The key to success in these and other collaborative arrangements is an organization's ability to clearly define its goals and realistically assess whether or not it has the capability to achieve them alone.

Collaborative policy development

As federal and state policy issues become increasingly complex, groups that used to lobby independently have learned they can be more effective by working together. Bankers, real estate agents, savings and loan executives and brokerage representatives have found they can be more effective if they can identify and work on policy issues together rather than independently. Manufacturers of all kinds are drawn together to work on foreign trade issues, just as health care executives, insurance representatives, doctors, hospitals and businesses have found they can be more effective if they work together to improve health care policy. Similarly, educators and business people are working together to define policies which will improve schools.

Collaborative research and development

Collaborative efforts are also increasingly common in research and development activities. Individual organizations are often constrained by capital restrictions as well as pressures on cash flow, time, people and the need to produce short-term results. These pressures frequently make it difficult to undertake research and development activities companies know they should address. Rather than not doing the work, firms have formed alliances. The Gas Research Institute (GRI) was established to undertake research and development programs that benefit the entire gas industry. GRI manages projects that usually have several characteristics: they are beyond the capabilities of any single member company; they require financial resources beyond what an individual company may want to spend; and/or they are sufficiently futuristic or high risk that a single company would prefer not to undertake the work alone. The Electric Power

Research Institute (EPRI) does the same work for the electrical industry.

Collaborative product development
Collaborative efforts are also increasingly important in the design and development of new products or services. Within organizations these efforts are being organized around teams such as the one that developed the Ford Taurus. Apple Computer developed joint ventures with Sony that enabled both to produce the PowerBook 100 in fewer than 13 months. John Scully, chairman of Apple, summed up the company's new attitude when he observed, "We learned in the 1980s we can't do it alone."[124]

Collaborative marketing and sales
There are increasingly numerous joint efforts to improve marketing and sales. CBS and Coca-Cola teamed up to promote the 1992 Olympics with a $16 million "Watch and Win" promotion. Coca-Cola is teaming up with Nestle to produce ready-to-drink coffees and teas. Nestle can produce the product and Coca-Cola has the distribution system to sell it. Rather than duplicating arrangements that already exist, companies have found that they can do a better job by working with others who already have the capabilities they need. One of the more bizarre examples of these types of collaborative efforts is the marketing program being undertaken by Japanese bankers and undertakers to develop what they call "neighborly compassion." According to Hisaki Matsuura from the project: "If we can handle this well, we'll be able to establish eternal relationships."[125]

These alliances give companies with products better access to markets and usually do not interfere with internal operations.

Collaborative economic development
Following World War II, successful economic development was the result of individual businesses pursuing their own self-interest. When they were successful, communities benefited. This approach has given way to a realization that collaboration is essential. In the 1990s, successful economic development re-

quires close working relationships among business people, public officials and service providers such as school systems and hospitals. Because intelligence is now society's strategic resource and quality of life considerations are increasingly important, successful economic development activities mean people from different parts of a community have to work together. In Red Wing, Minn., 1,000 people participated in Red Wing 2000 — a community-wide effort to design the town's future. Under the leadership of former Mayor Joanelle Dyrsted (now the Lieutenant Governor of Minnesota), working groups of business people, educators, public officials, health care providers, community leaders and volunteers worked together to plan for the economic future. Individuals and groups developed a shared vision of their community's future, and the steps needed to realize their goals.

Collaborative resolution of disputes

In 1991, the Colorado Bar Association became the nation's first State Bar Association to endorse a rule that lawyers should inform their clients of alternatives to litigation. The traditional legal system is based on the idea that truth will emerge from an adversarial process in which antagonists present their own views and challenge the views of their opponents. The difficulty with this approach is that in many cases it can be more damaging than useful, particularly in the cases in which resolving the issue is more important than assessing blame. In some cases, litigation is too expensive and people can't afford the costs. In others, the traditional legal system exacerbates difficulties among people who have to continue their relationship even though they may have had a serious dispute — a circumstance inherent in divorce proceedings and many small business disputes.

Alternative mechanisms based on the idea that we can work together have significant benefits. The CIGNA Insurance Company found that using arbitration significantly reduced both the time and cost of resolving disputes. CIGNA estimated that using arbitration rather than jury trials reduced the time necessary to resolve an issue from 42 months to nine months and further reduced attorney's fees from $8,000 to $2,400.[126] Alternatives to the traditional legal system are based on the idea that resolving

■

the issue is more important than declaring the winner and, in many cases, these alternatives enable people to solve their differences and even maintain their relationships.

There are common themes in all of these efforts. First, they are based on a view of the world that values collaboration as much as it values independence. Second, they are based on a recognition of the growing importance of information, whether that information is embodied in reports, analysis or people dealing with each other in face-to-face working sessions.

Specialization and independence were helpful ideas during the industrial period; they led to a higher standard of living and many of the benefits we all enjoy today. It is now clear, however, that we have reached the limits of what can be accomplished without modifying these ideas and to developing our capability to work together.

■ COLLABORATION AND COMPETITION

"The goal isn't to reduce diversity to
conformity, it's to maximize harmony."
— *J. Daniel Beckum*[127]

Commitments to collaboration have produced some unusual arrangements. Apple and IBM are collaborating on the development of the next generation of computer software, while competing with each other to sell computers, software and services. At the same time, John Scully of Apple and Bill Gates of Microsoft have an even odder relationship. The two companies have joint ventures in some areas while they simultaneously pursue lawsuits against each other in areas unrelated to their collaborative work.[128] For people who believe the world should be orderly and logical, this is all a little odd.

The phenomenon of people and organizations competing and collaborating simultaneously shows up in other fields as well. Mastercard and Visa compete for new card holders, but collaborate on security systems and fraud as well as technical systems that enable their customers to use each other's ATMs. Book publishers compete for authors and markets, but collaborate on stocking and shipping arrangements. Truck lines and railroads collaborate on piggyback rail systems that enable trains to carry trucks while they simultaneously compete for customers.

These arrangements work because the people who design and manage them realize they have to find better ways to meet the needs of those they serve. In every case, participants realize they don't have to compete across the board and that collaboration can lead to bigger markets and more business. Restricting the number of ATMs that credit card holders can use hurts both Mastercard and Visa.

While there are clear benefits, we still often have problems working together. Retailers have trouble working collaboratively on economic development efforts because of their reluctance to change how they operate their individual businesses. Doctors frequently resist expanding medical staffs for fear it will hurt their practice. This inability to work together to expand a market rather than focus more narrowly on individual success almost always hurts more than it helps.

Antique dealers as well as car dealers have learned that by co-locating they can attract more people and then compete in a larger market. Individual store owners and department store chains have found they can be more successful by co-locating to attract customers and sharing the costs of rent, utilities and other operating expenses. Farmers have long used co-ops as a way to increase their individual success and reduce costs.

■ CHALLENGES AND OPPORTUNITIES

> "I may have to do it myself, but that doesn't mean I have to do it alone."
> — *Anonymous*

While there is a growing agreement on the value of collaboration, there are still significant challenges.

Past success

While there are benefits to developing these arrangements, there are also barriers, one of which is our individual and collective experiences. People who have been successful generally got where they are because of an ability to thrive in competitive, hierarchical systems. Building collaborative relationships requires different skills.

Past success, in and of itself, often frustrates our ability to develop collaborative arrangements because it reinforces habits that may have been helpful in the past, but are not helpful now and won't be in the future. The most difficult challenge is to overcome the argument that "what we're doing works — why should we change it?"

> "One reason our people weren't getting aboard earlier was the curse of success."
> — Roger Smith[129]

Success in a hierarchy was defined by a manager's ability to promote his or her own interests. Too many managers still think of cooperation as arrangements in which one person does the "co-ing," while the other does the "operating." People who can build and maintain collaborative efforts have the ability to bring others together, identify common themes, respond to different points of view and develop a commitment to broader goals and the work necessary to achieve them.

Egos

A second challenge to building collaborative arrangements has to do with ego. During negotiations to take over RJ Reynolds, two of the brokerage firms involved were unable to agree on who would get the credit for doing the deal. The argument boiled down to the very practical question of which underwriter's name would go on the prominent left side of the tombstone advertisement in the *Wall Street Journal*. Their focusing on who would get the credit rather than accomplishing the work was one factor that eventually resulted in a third party, Henry Kravis of Kohlberg Kravis Roberts & Company, assuming control of the company.[130]

The continuing inability of the Chicago Board of Trade and the Chicago Mercantile Exchange to merge their operations is another example of egos gone haywire. Patrick Arbor, a director of the Board of Trade, argues that "It makes so much sense for us to get together, but here we are fighting it out again — politics, the location of the office, institutional pride and who has to walk several blocks — are all barriers to the completion of the merger."[131] The benefits of a possible merger have, as this is being written, continued to be lost in petty squabbles about issues that are secondary and, in some cases, ludicrous.

Similar problems play out in other settings every day. Efforts to improve education by rearranging or consolidating school districts are blocked by feelings of community pride. Government agencies stumble over their preoccupation with preserving their own budgets and prestige rather than submerging these interests to achieve a broader public good. When all is said and done, the result of this preoccupation with egos is poor service, higher costs and lost opportunities.

■ BUILDING COLLABORATIVE RELATIONSHIPS

While there are clearly challenges to building collaborative relationships, we now have enough experience to understand what it takes to develop them successfully.

Corporate values and cultures

During the industrial period, we treated organizations as if they were all the same. Now it is becoming clearer that organizations, like people, have characteristics that vary widely and the opportunity to develop collaborative efforts is much greater when participants from organizations share similar values and attributes.

Partner's interests

Collaborative efforts don't work if they don't respond to the individual real needs of the people or organizations involved. Participants won't go through the additional time, trouble and work if the issue is seen as being secondary to their individual well being.

Timing

Collaborative efforts won't work if the timing is wrong. If one partner has to focus on immediate issues, building longer term collaborative efforts may be impossible. The issue may be valid and the work may be important, but if the timing is wrong it won't work.

Building collaborative efforts is a lot like dating. It helps to build the relationship carefully. The barriers can be overcome if it is clear about what they are and how they should be addressed.

Planning

Planning efforts are productive because they enable participants to consider future opportunities rather than the pressures of the moment. Focusing on the future makes it easier to find common goals and identify ways we can work together to achieve them. Planning work, whether it is among departments within a single organization or among an organization and its clients and/or vendors, invariably leads to closer working relationships and better results.

Marketing

Joint marketing efforts among airlines, hotels and car rental companies and similar efforts among communities and states to promote tourism are examples of the benefits of collaboration in marketing. These usually tend not to affect the operations of individual participants, but strengthen each partner's ability to attract customers and increase sales.

Operations

A growing number of companies find they can improve operations by working together rather than independently. Hospital purchasing programs and television stations sharing satellite news facilities are examples of collaborative operating agreements which make it possible to either improve services or reduce costs.

Human resource development

Training programs that address the common needs of different organizations are an easy and effective way to bring people together. Since most organizations already invest in training, the opportunity is to use existing time and resources more effectively. Since the time, people and resources are already committed, these efforts represent a significant opportunity to use existing resources more effectively.

Building collaborative efforts requires that we change our habits. Rather than focusing on just our own responsibilities, we will have to start spending time in other parts of our organizations and more time with clients, vendors and even people in other fields. We will have to take down the boundaries between departments and re-invent entire institutions. We have accomplished as much as we can by working alone; we will be able to accomplish more by working together.

PART TWO

ANTICIPATING
THE FUTURE

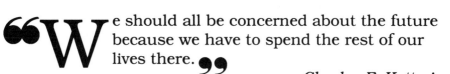e should all be concerned about the future
because we have to spend the rest of our
lives there.

          — *Charles F. Kettering*
          Seed for Thought, *1949*

DEVELOPING FORESIGHT

CHAPTER SEVEN

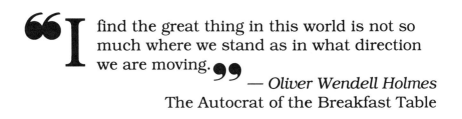

"I find the great thing in this world is not so much where we stand as in what direction we are moving.**"**
— *Oliver Wendell Holmes*
The Autocrat of the Breakfast Table

Inside...

■ The impact of change: preliminary lessons

■ Assessing future possibilities

■ THE IMPACT OF CHANGE: PRELIMINARY LESSONS

> "Tried and true means dead and buried."
> — *Brandon Tartikoff*
> *Entertainment Executive*[132]

Brandon Tartikoff's observation may be extreme, but it does have the value of encouraging us to think about what we do from a different perspective. We can always learn more — both about the issues discussed in part one and about others — if we are willing to examine patterns that underlie seemingly unrelated events. This willingness to learn from patterns and relationships is essential if we are to manage the future effectively.

People who successfully manage change have an ability to step back from the pressures of the moment and learn. They are open to new ideas and continuously look for patterns to help them anticipate the future. Some lessons are already clear.

Continuing old ways of doing things won't help or guide us

In the agricultural society, practical lessons of the past were reliable guides for the present and the future. Now, farmers grapple with the reality of an increasingly turbulent global economy. Companies such as ConAgra and Coca-Cola are exploring aquaculture with the expectation that early in the next century the oceans, rather than the land, will be our major source of food. Disney World is experimenting with hydroponics — growing plants in water — in the belief that such systems can be commercially viable within a decade. The genetic manipulation of animal breeds, a field dubbed "farmacy," will continue to grow.[133] Farmers and others are involved in debates about the appropriateness of genetically manipulating animals in addition to the usual political battles concerning land use, soil erosion and the effect of tax policy on the family farm.

Whatever the future of agriculture holds, many of the practical lessons of earlier generations no longer apply and what is true for farmers is true for all of us: regardless of what we do or where we live, relying on the ways we did things in the past is little help in planning the future.

We need to create the future, not defend the present

Over the past 50 years, energy issues and oil concerns specifically have become crucial issues to governments around the world.[134] In the United States, our dependence on oil and concerns about political instability in the Middle East are central issues in the broader debates about energy and how it is used. Debates concerning the merits and costs of superconductors, co-generation, solar and geothermal energy and conservation involve hundreds of thousands of people committed to the idea that we have to rethink how we use energy.

This push to develop cleaner alternatives isn't limited to environmentalists. British Petroleum (BP), one of the world's largest oil companies, has begun the research and development of much cleaner, less environmentally damaging fuels.[135] While energy issues are complex and politically charged, resisting broader and emerging possibilities because they force us to realign political and economic arrangements only delays their inevitable development.

The future will be great — next week, next month and next year will be difficult

We all face this dilemma. We all tend to think the future will be better than the present — it's getting from here to there that will be difficult. In health care, medical scientists routinely experiment with ground-breaking technologies, while health care providers simultaneously struggle with caring for the 38 million Americans without health insurance. Changes in health care payment systems, debates about rationing and the emergence of competition among and between doctors and hospitals have significantly altered the health care landscape. Doctors and health care executives trained to work in a regulated industry are now being forced to develop new management arrangements and at the same time, prepare for even greater changes to come.

Our growing ability to alter, manipulate, extend or terminate life suggests that health care professionals face a challenging decade. We know that health care in the future will be different from what it is today. The issue is how we get from here to there.

The rate of change will continue to accelerate

Perhaps no field exemplifies the accelerating rate of change as clearly as telecommunications. Bill Gates of Microsoft has "already invested six years and hundreds of millions of dollars in multimedia computing that integrates sound, moving pictures, and text all in a personal computer."[136]

This accelerating rate of change has led to the development of arrangements that would have been unthinkable in the past. AT&T is hiring senior executives from retailing, banking and other fields to help the company compete in an increasingly deregulated industry far different from its stable past.[137] Telephone and computer companies once operated in distinct and separate industries. Now traditional industry boundaries have blurred with AT&T's entry into the computer field and IBM's entry into communications. The pace of change in telecommunications may be more rapid than in other fields, but the reality of accelerating change and shifting industry boundaries is common to us all.

We have to redesign what we do and how we do it

During periods of stability we could safely continue business as usual, but during turbulent times, the risk of continuing old practices often is higher than the risks associated with change.

Our education systems are a good example of the need to assume the risks associated with change. In the industrial world, learning was desirable, but not essential. People could earn a good living without a strong education. In the information society, learning and education are critical and most of us can expect to spend a significant portion of our total lives learning.

While the world has changed around our educational institutions, most are still organized around the patterns and needs of earlier agricultural and industrial societies. The school calendar is organized around the rhythms of farm life even though fewer than 3 percent of us work on the land. The routines of school life reflect the orderliness and clear rules of the industrial society. The time for learning is from 9 a.m. to 3 p.m. The place is a schoolhouse and people who teach are certified.

These arrangements will give way to alternatives in which learning occurs in places such as community centers, office buildings, factory floors and churches, as well as schools. Learning will happen around the clock throughout the year and we will learn from people who have something to teach whether or not they are certified. Ideas such as vouchers, longer school years and performance standards for teachers are all parts of the ongoing debate about how schools operate. These discussions are significant not only because they are important in and of themselves, but because they are symbolic of the restructuring occurring in every part of society.

Habits of the past are often barriers to the future

Like executives in other fields, manufacturers struggle with the idea that the habits of the past are barriers to present survival for future prosperity. While the future of manufacturing will be different, work in the here and now focuses on shifting our emphasis from high-volume to flexible production systems which enable us to adapt products to changing customer preferences. Some examples of how to achieve this already exist. Panasonic produces bicycle models in any one of 11,231,862 different configurations (including 18 models and 199 colors) that conform to their customers' individual body shapes and riding styles — and does it within two days.[138]

The last decade has been difficult for people unwilling to change their habits. Managing successfully requires that we examine our habits from the perspective of whether they will be useful in the future rather than whether they were helpful in the past.

We need to think about things differently

One approach to dealing with the future is to think about issues from the standpoint of someone who may see it differently, whether it is a customer, a vendor or an interested observer. A second is to think through an issue from a perspective opposite from the one we might naturally embrace. If we thought our idea was a good one, what would someone who disagreed say?

Another way to think about emerging issues is to consider them from the perspective of a different point in time. How would someone view what we did if they were looking back from a point 20 years in the future? Thinking about issues from the perspective of the future is a helpful way to clarify what matters as well as a useful way to avoid being caught up in the pressures of the whirlwind. If we think about our lives from this perspective, a number of questions surface:

- What kind of work will I be doing 10 years from now?
- What will I be learning?
- How will I learn?
- What will I believe?
- In what ways will I find satisfaction?
- What will worry me most?
- What will I hope for?
- What personal relationships will matter to me most?

There are similar questions that relate to organizations.

- How will we measure success?
- What will my division be doing 10 years from now?
- What will we do in the future that we don't do now?

- What do we do now that we won't do in the future?
- How will we provide value to people we serve?
- How will we spend our time?
- What will a typical day look like?

While asking these kinds of questions doesn't guarantee success, thinking about them provides perspective which can help us manage, rather than be victimized by, change we experience.

∎ ASSESSING FUTURE POSSIBILITIES

"When a society breaks dramatically with the past, when idols and heroes are overthrown, it's like a dust storm. It's difficult to see what will emerge in the end."
— *Mikhail Gorbachev*

The future may be different from the present but that doesn't mean it has to be either surprising or mysterious. The difficulty is that too many of us see only what lies immediately ahead rather than what lies further on or off to the side. The reality of continuous change is that what we consider offbeat today may be tomorrow's reality. Early environmental advocates were attacked as mindless idealists and many corporations argued that energy conservation would ruin their business. Now the 3M Corporation has management performance standards to achieve energy savings. And, a growing number of businesses use conservation or co-generation techniques to reduce their energy use.

Assessing the impact of potential future developments is an essential part of managing the future. If the steel industry, for example, had been willing to look at the future open-mindedly, it might have been spared significant pain. Companies and unions might have embraced new technologies and alternative production systems and, in doing so, avoided layoffs and plant closings that plagued the industry for years. The lesson is that assessing what could happen in the future based on the present or the past will, more often than not, get us in trouble. Phrases such as "that will never happen" or "we don't have to worry about ..." are sure signs of trouble. Similarly, responding to emerging possibilities as if they were "yes or no" choices precludes our ability to explore what they might mean in a future which is different from the present. Tomorrow's major issues all have their roots in the present and they all have characteristics we can assess to determine how they might affect us.

Scope

Every issue has a scope that may be local, regional, national or global. Changes in financial markets, for example, are global. They touch us all. Political turmoil in Haiti is regional and may affect public policy in Florida, but is less likely to affect state policy in Montana. Sales of foreign cars are higher on the coasts than they are in middle America. The impact of an aging population varies by region across the country. We hear about so many issues every day that focusing on an issue's scope is one way to sort out the important from the unimportant.

Time frame

The timing of potential future developments is a second consideration in determining how it might affect us. Legislative actions, regulatory hearings and judicial proceedings usually have a short-term impact, while questions of bioethics, the creation of artificial life and manufacturing in outer space will affect us in a more distant future.

To manage the future effectively, we have to make judgments about which issues require immediate attention, which may affect us in the near future, approximately five years or so and which may affect us in the longer term, a decade or more into the future. The better our understanding of when an issue may affect us, the easier it is to determine how we should deal with it.

Likelihood

A third consideration is the extent to which any given issue is actually likely to occur and assess whether its likelihood is low, medium or high. Looking back we clearly underestimated the likelihood of Japan and Germany benefiting from the Marshall Plan. Another example occurred during the 1950s and 1960s, when we underestimated the likelihood of the women's movement becoming a major social force. In both cases, we were aware of the issue but didn't think efforts to develop Japan and Germany or promote women's issues would be successful.

In most cases, our inability to accurately gauge the likelihood of an issue affecting us is the result of being caught up in the forces of the whirlwind. The not surprising result is that we become captives of the present and lose our ability to consider how future developments may affect us.

Impact

Similarly, the impact of an issue may vary from low to high. If the potential impact of an issue is low, we can ignore it. If it is high, we better deal with it. Ethics and integrity, for example, have become major concerns in the financial service industry. This was reflected in decisions by some pension fund managers to end their relationships with Salomon Brothers following the firm's abuse of federal regulations on the auctioning of treasury bonds.[139] Salomon executives, who knew federal laws were being violated, could have foreseen that sooner or later illegal trading practices would explode in public. Ignoring the issue and refusing to take action to correct abuses of both the customer's trust and the law assured eventual public exposure and subsequent criminal charges.

To determine the potential impact of an issue, we have to view it from the perspective of what it might mean rather than whether or not we are in favor of it.

During periods of stability we can focus on our jobs and when we have time, think about the future. The dimensions of change we experience now mean our priorities have to change.

Evaluating the future and assessing the potential impact of emerging issues is an essential part of our work.

The Power of Ideas:

Paradigms and Paradigm Shifts

Chapter Eight

66 A social paradigm is a constellation of values, beliefs and experiences that enable people to work together and communicate with one another with some degrees of success. **99**

— *Joseph T. Plummer*[140]

Inside...

- How ideas change: The phases of a paradigm shift

- Five ideas that shape our lives

- Dealing with paradigm shifts

■ THE POWER OF IDEAS: PARADIGMS AND PARADIGM SHIFTS

"Everyone behaves in accordance with a theory ... whether or not they are aware of it."

— *Peter Drucker*

Underlying the way we deal with practical issues are ideas that shape our behavior and it is these ideas about the world and how it works that determine how we behave.

Our perceptions of time are a good example of how ideas shape our behavior. The rising young executive obsessed with the pressures of the moment reflects, most likely unconsciously, a belief that time moves forward and the moment once past is lost forever. Advertisements for Reebok — "Life is short, play hard" — reinforce the same idea. While the belief that time moves forward was one of the significant organizing ideas of the industrial society, it would have been alien to earlier generations. In the agricultural society, people believed time was circular. It couldn't be lost or wasted because there would always be another planting and another harvest. New opportunities came with each new season and the seasons themselves followed each other in never ending cycles.

While ideas such as time moving forward shape our behavior, we rarely talk about them. We don't turn to friends at cocktail parties, baseball games or company meetings and ask what they think of linear time. Nor are we likely to ask what they think about survival of the fittest, the single unifying theory or evolutionary change. We talk instead about individual decisions and events rather than the ideas that underlie them. As long as our decisions reflect widely shared ideas, we can act in ways that are understandable to each other. Conversely, when people act on the basis of differing ideas, there is inevitably confusion, difficulty and even conflict.[141]

One helpful way to think about the effect of ideas on how we behave is Thomas Kuhn's work on paradigms and paradigm shifts.[142] In his book, *The Structure of Scientific Revolutions*, Kuhn describes the process of scientific change. He defined paradigms as the world views or models of reality. Paradigms are the ideas we all "know" to be right. They are important because they shape our expectations and behavior. Believing time is linear, for example, leads to a preoccupation with the present, almost to the exclusion of an interest in the past or future. Like the children's story of the Three Little Pigs, we are too often willing to build houses of straw to meet the needs of the moment rather than take the time to build what is durable and what will serve us well in the future.

Kuhn called the process by which we change ideas a "paradigm shift" and although he was writing about scientific change, his thoughts are helpful as a way to think about other changes as well.[143] Kuhn suggested that paradigm shifts occur in three phases. The first is a period of debate during which we challenge ideas we previously accepted. To use a popularized example, we used to believe "a woman's place was in the home." Now, bumper stickers tell us that a woman's place "is in the House — and the Senate." In the second phase of a paradigm shift, things break down. Concepts we previously accepted no longer accurately describe reality. Further, systems we have developed to meet our needs no longer work as effectively as they did in the past. In the third phase, the period of developing alternatives, we are willing to consider ideas and ways of doing things we previously rejected. Our willingness to allow private companies to manage public services such as airports and garbage removal are examples.

People who argue that we have always had change and that what we are experiencing now is nothing new miss Kuhn's point. The nature of change during periods of stability is qualitatively different from the changes we experience during a paradigm shift. During periods of stability, change occurs within the existing set of rules. We accept, for example, the idea that bigger is better and, more importantly, the thought that questions of scale are a useful and important way to think about the world. During a paradigm shift we challenge the rules themselves.

■ HOW IDEAS CHANGE: THE PHASES OF A PARADIGM SHIFT

> "Faced with having to change our views or prove that there is no need to do so, most of us get busy on the proof."[144]
> — *John Kenneth Galbraith*

Debates

We have always had debates, and in all likelihood we always will. Reaching agreement is hard enough when people are operating within the same set of rules. It is much more difficult, if not impossible, when we see the world differently. Kuhn argued that during this period of debate people's ideas are often so different that they are frequently unable to even communicate. People who believe the world is logical and change occurs slowly have difficulty talking with people who think it is messy and change happens quickly. This commitment to a logical world is symbolized by the phrase, "I'll believe it when I see it." This idea may have been useful in the industrial society, but is not helpful now. Accepting new ideas requires embracing new paradigms. Today, the catch phrase becomes "I'll see it when I believe it."[145] The motion picture industry's reaction to the growth of video tape machines is a good example of this phenomenon. Studio executives believed renting movies so people could watch them at home would ruin their business. The people who developed the business believed in it and as a result developed a multi-million dollar industry which benefited both groups.

These challenges to existing paradigms come from people who question prevailing thoughts about how the world works.

The economist, Lester Thurow, former dean of the Sloan Business School at Massachusetts Institute of Technology, argues that existing economic theory is seriously flawed because economic theories no longer predict reality.[146] Thurow uses a sailing analogy and discusses the need to abandon a beautiful sailing ship in favor of a raft. The raft won't have the beauty or elegance of the sailing ship, but it has one undeniably valuable feature — it floats.[147] Thurow's point is that we need to rethink economic theory — an argument that frequently irritates colleagues committed to traditional economics. These seemingly abstract economic theories affect us all through, for example, the behavior of the stock market. Because traditional market theories no longer adequately explain the behavior of the stock market, Wall Street brokerage firms now routinely hire "quants." These people are statistical wizards who analyze financial markets using concepts such as chaos theory rather than traditional economics.

The challenge during periods of debate centers on our willingness to re-examine deeply held beliefs. The difficulty inherent in debating strongly held beliefs is compounded by the fact that as we move through a paradigm shift even the words we use mean different things to different people.[148] Different definitions of the family, for instance, translate into differing views on issues such as whether or not we should publicly finance daycare programs. People committed to what we think of as the traditional family tend to oppose publicly funded daycare. People committed to what we think of as the non-traditional families — those headed by a single parent or families in which both adults work — tend to support publicly financed daycare. There are endless examples of the difficulty of resolving issues when the meaning of words is unclear. Political debates about regulation in the financial services industry, for example, are increasingly complex, in part because we have differing perceptions of what a bank is or should be.

This period of debate is especially frustrating for people who cling to old paradigms and require clarity to be comfortable. These people are likely to be increasingly frustrated because their attempts to impose order will invariably be ineffective. Open-mindedness and a willingness to explore new possibilities are essential to obtain a view of beyond the moment and envision what might be possible in a different future.

Breakdowns

The second phase of a paradigm shift is the most difficult for most of us to accept. We have to accept the idea that the arrangements that once served us well are no longer effective. In the words of Marvin Harris, "America has become a land plagued by loose wires, missing screws, things that don't fit, things that don't last and things that don't work."[149] If we choose to acknowledge them, signs of breakdowns are all around us and, unfortunately, some of the clearest examples have to do with a breakdown in values. Beechnut Foods diluted baby food in what Assistant U.S. Attorney Thomas H. Rouch called "a classic case of big corporate greed and irresponsibility,"[150] television evangelists spend as much or more time raising money as they do promoting religion,[151] and violence is everywhere when even children carry guns to school.

This breakdown in values is compounded by breakdowns in the systems we use every day. A surprising number of hospital bills are inaccurate.[152] A funeral home in New York almost cremated a nursing home patient, because employees mistakenly thought she was dead. In the airline industry, "pencil whipping" is the culprit. This involves doctoring computer entries, log books, and work cards so maintenance and safety records erroneously provide the appearance that the work has been performed.[153] Some breakdowns are serious, others are serious and humorous, as well. An enterprising toll booth attendant in Palm Gardens, Florida, was able to run her own "independent" toll booth and collect about $15,000 before she was caught.[154] Another woman who became known as "Robin Hud" set up her own foundation to help the needy. She may have had good intentions, but her source of funds was millions of dollars she had stolen from her employer, the Department of Housing and Urban Development.[155]

If these were isolated incidents, we could argue they were regrettable, but certainly not cause for alarm. The unfortunate

■

reality is that they are simply the more visible examples of the breakdowns Kuhn described. One reason it's hard to deal with the breakdown phase of a paradigm shift is that it's impossible to solve a problem we won't acknowledge. The arguments we use to deny the breakdown are almost always the same:

- "The problem is an exception. It happens rarely and we shouldn't worry about it." This is usually incorrect. The problems are frequently more widespread than we are willing to admit and, all too often, we ignore both the reality and the messenger who brings the news.
- The reaction, "We don't do things like that," is almost always made as a flat statement and it is usually wrong. Denying the problem makes it impossible to fix.
- "It's against policy." This argument is usually right, but irrelevant. A policy that isn't followed isn't a policy.
- "It's not us, they did it." The inclination that other people need to change underlies our inability to accept that we, rather than they, may need to address these breakdowns.
- "That's the way things are." We have become so accustomed to poor service and shoddy products that we simply accept them.

What is striking about contemporary criticism of how things work is that it is coming from mainstream leaders rather than what we used to call fringe elements such as the discontented, hippies or perpetual pessimists who, we argued, would invariably find fault with everything. James C. Miller, Ronald Reagan's, Director of the Office of Management and Budget, stated that, "the budget process in the United States simply doesn't work."[156] Barry Goldwater, one of the country's most distinguished conservatives, explained that the problem with the United States Congress is that "they don't have the guts to do what they ought to do."[157] Ernest Boyer, the head of the Carnegie Foundation for the Advancement of Teaching, says, "The undergraduate college, the very heart of higher learning, is a troubled institution."[158] We may have been able to shrug off criticism when it came from the fringes, but denial is harder when the critics are our leaders.

∎

Part of our difficulty in accepting that systems are breaking down derives from the fact that the systems we are attacking now served us well for over 50 years. During the early part of this century, our expectations were clear and most organizations met or exceeded our hopes. Increasing enrollments in the American educational system, the availability of affordable housing, improved health care and the development of products and services that improved our quality of life were the result of widely shared paradigms and our ability to act on what we believed.

Unfortunately too many of us still believe that doing more of what we have always done will make the system work. Once we accept the idea that many of our systems are beyond repair, we can begin to change them. By viewing the present realistically, we will be able to preserve what is sound, discard what doesn't work and move on to create better arrangements to meet our needs.

Alternatives

While the second phase of a paradigm shift is frustrating and difficult, the third is exciting and positive. We are willing to entertain new concepts and explore different methods. Caution and certainty give way to "ready, fire, aim."[159]

This willingness to explore new possibilities is everywhere. In the academic world, physicists are exploring areas such as "string theory" — the idea that there may be 10, rather than four, dimensions to our experience; [160] historians explore fields such as "psycho-history" and biogeneticists and philosophers explore the human mind.

This willingness to explore and experiment is evident beyond the university as well. It shows up in the development of new insurance products, new financial products and newspapers such as *USA Today*. Every year there are over 9,000 new products introduced in the grocery store. This example is reflective of developments in almost every other field.

Not only are we developing new products and services, we are also increasingly willing to test new ways to produce them.

Words such as participatory management and quality reflect our willingness to consider new ways to arrange work.

Historically, the phases of a paradigm shift occurred slowly and sequentially; now they are occurring simultaneously. The result is often confusion and an inability to escape the forces of the whirlwind. By stepping back and thinking both about how ideas change and what ideas are changing we can anticipate rather than react to changes that will affect us in the future.

■ FIVE IDEAS THAT SHAPE OUR LIVES

> "A true voyage consists of seeing familiar
> lands through new eyes."
> — *Marcel Proust*[161]

One striking characteristic of our present is that paradigms are changing in a variety of ways simultaneously. This pervasiveness of change is reflected in how our views about change and stability, the environment, the importance of the past, the value of experience, as well as our ideas about religion, philosophy and art in society, are all shifting. The result is changing expectations for our relationships, work and organizations.

Change and stability

Charles Darwin's ideas about evolutionary change were the basis for a paradigm that enjoyed extraordinary support for over a hundred years. Now, we must face alternative ideas about how change occurs. Biologists Niles Eldredge and Steven J. Gould have advanced a theory of "punctuated equilibrium." This concept maintains that evolution occurs in fits and starts rather than as a continuous flow of small changes.[162] Richard Foster, a director of the consulting firm McKinsey and Company, has advanced the same idea in a business context. Foster argues that in addition to evolutionary change there are "step changes" — periods of stability followed by periods of rapid development in repeating cycles — and total disruption is the development of entire new technologies or industries in a very short time.[163]

If change rather than stability is the permanent condition, then, as John Teets of the Greyhound Corporation describes it, our responsibility is to guide the forces of change.[164] Koji Kobayashi, Chairman Emeritus of the NEC Corporation, speaks to a paradox inherent in our ideas about change and stability when he notes, "A stable company is unstable and an unstable one is stable. A company that realizes it is unstable will do its utmost to achieve stability. A stable company, on the other hand, becomes unstable through its attempts to preserve the status quo."[165] There is another paradox. During a paradigm shift, the slower we go, the faster we move. To act effectively, we have to first take the time to build a common understanding of what we want to do. Too often we rush to make decisions, but little changes because the people involved continue to have different views about what ought to be done.

Over the next decade, success will come to those who are willing to manage change rather than defend stability. In the words of Jack Welch, chairman of General Electric, if the rate of change inside an institution is less than the rate of change outside, the end is in sight.

The environment

The early Greeks and Romans believed nature was sacred. They lived in a pantheistic world and believed that their gods were embodied in the trees, water, and sky. Neptune was god of the sea and Diana the goddess of the hunt. These beliefs meant that nature had to be protected, because, as the social observer Jeremy Rifkin points out, "people don't destroy their gods."[166]

By the 1700s, we had embraced the idea of a single god embodied in our souls and the heavens rather than nature. As a result, Rene Descartes, one of the period's eminent philosophers, could write that one significant characteristic of human existence was our ability to master and possess nature.[167] This paradigm enabled the developers of the industrial society to exploit nature and develop many of the products we take for granted today — everything from pop-top soda cans to lunar landing modules.

Now our ideas about the environment are changing again. There is a growing acceptance of the idea that we need to manage the natural world with care. The belief that natural resources are finite and need to be preserved is reflected in the actions of governments, public and private organizations and many of us individually. The United Nations Conference on the Environment and the United States Environmental Protection Agency reflect a governmental commitment to preserving the environment. Private sector companies have begun to recycle or use environmentally sound materials. McDonald's, for example, has switched from Styrofoam to paper boxes and reduced its plastic waste by almost 90 percent.[168]

The emerging paradigm is based on the idea that we need to strike a balance with nature. This idea will be one of the strongest forces of the coming decade. Our belief in the importance of preserving the environment will shape our personal behavior and how we manage our organizations.

Preoccupation with the past

Like Darwin, Sigmund Freud had an extraordinary impact on how we view the world. Freud's belief that our adult lives are shaped by the forces of our childhood had the effect of turning our attention to the past. Freudian psychiatrists, as well as members of support groups such as Alcoholics Anonymous and Adult Children of Alcoholics, believe that understanding the past is key to dealing with the present and the future. While there is value to this idea, there are problems when the past becomes the dominant focus of our lives. Looking backward makes focusing on the future difficult, and emphasizing the past, the exclusion of the present or the future clouds our ability to see opportunities for change or what may lie ahead. The solution is not to ignore the past, but rather to draw thoughtfully on the lessons of history to help us manage the present and shape the future.

Data and experience

One of the great insights of the 1600s was that organizing data and experience could help us understand the world. Rene Descartes is generally acknowledged as the founder of what we now know as the scientific method. Three hundred years later, his conviction that we could understand the world by examining its component parts still affects much of what we do. The problem we face now is that we have gone too far. In his book, *The Fifth Discipline*, Peter Senge correctly argues that in focusing on details we lose our ability to see the big picture. In many instances, we are so overcome by the details that we lose sight of what actually matters — a phenomenon one friend described as being so focused on the ants that we don't see the elephants coming over the hill.

Debates in the 1960s and 1970s concerning the importance of raising children and the economic value of women who stayed home are good examples. Instead of examining factors such as ethics, values and the importance of children, we began churning out quantitative economic analyses concerning the value of a mother's work. We calculated the cost of ironing, dish washing, and fixing a meal to justify the value of women remaining in the home and raising children. The whole exercise was ludicrous. Our commitment to children is a function of values and common sense, not dollars.

Our preoccupation with reductionist thought — the idea that by understanding the parts, we understand the whole — often is more harmful than helpful. Organizations add staff to perform work that seems essential if we focus on the details, but less valuable if we look at the organization's overall goals. Health care policy focuses on reimbursement rates rather than on how we should provide for each other. And manufacturers who decide that producing quality products is too expensive miss the point that meeting the needs of customers is a much more important criterion for success.

Numbers may help our understanding, but they can never substitute for common sense. Over the next decade, success will come to those who focus on the missions of their organizations rather than to bean counters who focus only on the details.

Religion, philosophy and art

Over the past 200 years, there has been a steady movement towards thinking of religion, philosophy and art as the province of believers, artists, thinkers, and specialists. Removing ourselves from discussions of ethics and the meaning of history eventually leads to the never-never land in which anything is acceptable. In the 1990s, too many business people steal and too many school children carry guns. The positive side is that we can regain our sense of values. One interesting phenomenon is how moments of crisis can lead to an epiphany among even the most hardened souls. When Lee Atwater, the former head of the Republican Party, contracted cancer and faced death, his views about appropriate political behavior changed and he apologized to Michael Dukakis for what Atwater called his own "naked cruelty." In the 1988 campaign, following Watergate, dirty tricksters Charles Colson and Jeb McGruder, turned from politics to religion.

When John Donne wrote in the 1600s that, "No man is an island,"[169] he put his finger on a core reality of our existence. Culture, the integrated pattern of human knowledge, belief and behavior, shapes what is or is not acceptable and touches all of us. Sean Dowse, the executive director of the Sheldon Auditorium in Red Wing, Minn., talks about the importance of the arts and argues that our cultural values and ethical systems are as important as plumbing and sewage systems.

Over the coming decade, we will see a resurgence in the importance of values and ethics in our personal and professional lives. We will try to narrow the gap between what we believe and how we act. We will support those organizations and individuals who act on the basis of a commitment to a higher set of beliefs rather than their own narrow interests.

◼ DEALING WITH PARADIGM SHIFTS

"You can't drive to the future looking in the rear view mirror."
— *Buckminster Fuller*

During periods of stability, the ideas we accept have demonstrated their usefulness. There is no urgency to think about paradigms or the effect of ideas on how we behave.

During a paradigm shift, however, the situation is different. We have to be willing to explore ideas. How we think about time or questions about values and ethics become increasingly important. For people who pride themselves on being action-oriented, developing a willingness to re-examine what we previously took for granted is difficult. The idea that what worked in the past may not work in the future is hard to accept, especially for those who have been successful. It is a truism that people are willing to seek personal help when their worlds have collapsed and organizations are willing to change when they are bankrupt. There are fewer examples of people or organizations being willing to change when they are healthy.

Learning

The value of exploring ideas is valuable because it gives us the opportunity to learn and re-examine ideas we usually take for granted.

We can spend more time studying, especially outside our own fields. During periods of stability, our attention is on an increasingly specialized understanding of developments within our own fields. Just the opposite is true during a paradigm shift. Since the rules are changing, we must learn more about how other people see the world. Exploring ideas in areas such as ethics, physics, biology or economics may not be required, but it certainly can be helpful.

New experiences

We can also learn by seeking out new experiences. Whether these experiences occur on the job or during our leisure time is less important than the overall need to vary our experiences. Consciously changing what we do on the job, who we spend time with, or where we travel provides the opportunity to think about issues differently.

Managing change

We used to be in the business of maintaining systems; now all of us are in the business of managing change. There has been a perception that leaders handle change and the rest of us simply do our jobs. The reality now is that all of us are in the business of managing change and the final chapter suggests ways we can do it.

MANAGING THE WHIRLWIND

CHAPTER NINE

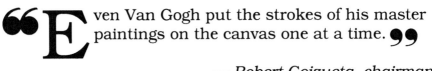

"Even Van Gogh put the strokes of his master paintings on the canvas one at a time.**"**

— Robert Goizueta, chairman
Coca-Cola

Inside...

■ Grasp of reality

■ Values

■ A vision of the future

■ Blocks to new ideas

■ Moving to a different future

■ A final story

■ MANAGING THE WHIRLWIND

"If America is going to prosper in the future
it has to change now."
— *Lester Thurow*[170]

The reality of change means we are going to have to think and behave differently if we are to manage, rather than be victimized by, forces that affect us.

■ GRASP OF REALITY

"If wishes were horses, beggars would ride."
— *Anonymous*

A grasp of reality is an essential requirement for success. The issue is not whether we like the changes we see but rather that the changes taking place are real. In the post war period, we could focus on immediate issues and know that the path in front of us would be more of the same. Like driving across Kansas, the highway would be straight and clear. Now, a grasp of reality requires that we discard that notion and focus our attention on two broad areas.

The first is continuing change in the social, economic and political fabric of the country. We get into trouble when we say things like, "they've never done that," "it won't happen," "not in this business," "we never have," "it's a fad," or "I don't believe it will happen." These phrases, and others like them, suggest the future will be more of the present. It won't. To manage the future we need to ask questions such as: What does it mean? How could it affect us? Will it grow or fade away? What could happen next? To argue that a particular situation is more of the same is to miss the uniqueness of our present environment. Patterns such as the growing importance of information and the need for collaboration hold opportunity, if we are willing to embrace, rather than resist, them.

Second, we have to accept the idea that most of our organizations fall short of realizing their potential. A grasp of reality requires that we understand an organization's strengths, weaknesses and individual eccentricities. Further, it means that executives and managers need to see their responsibilities in terms of the need to redesign and improve the organizations for which they are responsible.

On an individual level, this grasp of reality requires that each of us understand our own gifts and limitations so that we can identify skills and areas that we can build on as well as areas that require strengthening.

■ VALUES

> "Forget money and power ... This whole experience has taught me something new abut love, family, and mankind in general."
> — *Lee Atwater*[171]

Having spent the last 200 years focusing on the practical world of day-to-day events rather than questions of ethics and values, we are now shifting direction. Robert W. Fogel, an economic historian at the University of Chicago, argues that "moral issues are increasingly becoming the political issues of our age."[172] Author Thomas Moore believes "the great malady of the 20th Century is "loss of soul."[173]

This growing concern about values is reflected in a variety of ways. Professor Phillip Heyman Ames of the Harvard Law School writes that "law in the United States is often a game played by well equipped professionals against ill equipped amateurs and ... any such game is unfair."[174] House Speaker Tom Foley says members of Congress will now pay their own traffic tickets or go to court to settle the dispute themselves.[175] Rob Pilatus, a singer in the rock group Milli Vanilli, said the group was "seduced ...

and felt very guilty" when it was revealed they had not actually sung on their records which sold seven million copies and won a Grammy Award.[176]

Companies such as Johnson and Johnson thrive in no small measure because of their values. Johnson and Johnson's handling of the Tylenol poisonings in the 1980s was a dramatic and visible example of the company's willingness to act on behalf of its customers' interest. Johnson and Johnson pulled $8 million worth of products off shelves. The remarkable development was that following the poisonings, they were able to regain market share in one of the most competitive industries in the country. Anita Roddick, founder of a cosmetic company called The Body Shop, speaks from success when she observes that, "increasingly, consumers are looking to purchase products from companies that are more responsible."[177]

On a broader level, organizations are finding they can do well by doing right. Ironically, Shearson Lehman was less successful financially when it violated Treasury rules than when it followed them. The growing interest in values and concern for people with whom we work is reflected in the challenge to use the tools and technologies of the information society in ways that enable us to act in concert with the values of the earlier agricultural society. Our success in the future will be in part a function of how well we embrace traditional values such as caring about other people, whether they are people we serve or people with whom we work.

■ A VISION OF THE FUTURE

"Vision is the art of seeing things invisible."
— *Jonathon Swift*
Thoughts on Various Subjects[178]

There is a saying among planners that if you don't care where you're going, you're not lost. The idea is that without a vision of the future, anything we do is fine because if there is no goal there are no standards and anything is acceptable. A vision of the future provides focus for what we need to do and serves as a measure against which we can assess our progress. Unlike an operating plan, a vision is qualitative not quantitative. It is a description of attributes that shape behavior.

General Electric, under Jack Welch, has a clear and compelling vision of a premier corporation that is "boundaryless" and a dominant force in the markets it serves. Johnson & Johnson is driven by the vision embodied in its credo — the company's statement of its beliefs.[179] Memorial Healthcare System has a vision of a clinically and administratively integrated health care systems organized to meet the needs of patients in communities it serves. Goodhue County National Bank has a vision of itself as a community development organization. By strengthening the communities in which it operates, the bank will prosper, but the reverse may not be true.

Sometimes these visions of the future are more intuitive. Fred Smith developed Federal Express because he believed he could provide a valuable service and successfully compete with the post office. Steven Jobs and Stephen Wozniak believed people would use computers in their homes and that Apple could compete with IBM.

A vision of the future is critical because it enables the management of forces of the whirlwind. The absence of a vision leaves us captives of the pressures of the moment.

■ BLOCKS TO NEW IDEAS

> "There is no opportunity so great we can't find a way to avoid it."
>
> — *Pogo*

The question before us is how gracefully and effectively we can manage the transition from the present to a continuously changing future. To manage change successfully, we will have to deal with both changing ideas and practical issues simultaneously. And as often as not, practical issues cause us as much

■

difficulty as changing ideas. Dealing with change is tough, exemplified, somewhat humorously, by the spokesperson at Brooks Brothers who said the traditional clothing store's executives "sweated bullets" when they widened men's trouser legs from 16 inches to 17 inches 15 years ago.[180] Their anxiety reoccurred when they put escalators in their flagship store on Madison Avenue in New York. When referring to escalators, a Brooks Brothers spokesperson commented, "Let me tell you, we were worried. This is not a retail store, it's an American institution, and anything remotely revolutionary will destroy it."[181]

Other issues are more serious, more difficult and much more sensitive. A Tennessee Court of Appeals had to determine who had custody of two frozen embryos after the couple who created them divorced.[182] Still other changes highlight the ongoing conflict between the present and the future. The Celestes Corporation offers a service. It transports cremated remains into permanent orbit fifteen hundred miles above the earth. The difficulty is that in Florida, where the company is located, there are laws requiring all cemeteries to have at least fifteen acres of land and a paved road. According to Celestes president, John Cherry, "The company has to convince the state that we're in a difficult situation. We're not a cemetery, but a post-cremation transportation company."[183]

In each of these situations and countless others the theme isn't whether or not there will be change, but how we will manage it because our habits make it hard to embrace new ideas. Consciously or unconsciously, we block their development usually in any one or more of the following ways.

Premature and uninformed judgments

Too many of us often reach premature or uninformed judgments about issues we really don't understand. Financial professionals dismissed the cash management account developed by Bank One and Merrill Lynch in the 1970s because they believed it would never be accepted. Cash management accounts have since become one of the most successful financial products ever introduced. The tendency to reach premature judgments eliminates potential opportunities before we've even had a chance to explore their significance. This may save time and energy, but during periods of rapid change it leads to lost opportunities at exactly the moment we can least afford them.

Embarrassment

Our fear of being embarrassed often blocks our ability to act on new ideas. Most managers were trained to believe they should know the answers and during the industrial period it was probably a reasonable expectation. Now, because change affects all of us simultaneously, managers struggle along with the rest of us but too often are afraid to admit it. This fear of embarrassment is a problem for two reasons. First, some people deal with embarrassment by staying quiet and their silence makes it difficult to tell what they understand. Second, people who feel embarrassed are reluctant to wade into unfamiliar issues. In either case, the embarrassment is unnecessary because none of us knows what the future may hold. An alternative to feeling embarrassed is to accept the reality that each of us individually and all of us together are embarked on creating that different future.

Caution

Caution is a legitimate consideration in assessing new possibilities, but it is not a legitimate reason to stand still, avoid decisions or duck difficult issues. The premium on acting rapidly continues to go up. IBM was slow to develop personal computers and Xerox was slow to react to foreign competitors. In these cases and others, companies that move slowly, get hurt.

Uncertainty and demands for predictability

One paradox inherent in periods of uncertainty is that as the world becomes increasingly turbulent our demands for predictability go up. Paralysis by analysis becomes a common malady. Rather than learning how to manage innovation and minimize risk, we demand certainty. We want more analysis, more numbers and more guarantees. Not surprisingly, this makes it harder to take advantage of emerging possibilities. The Xerox Corporation's role in developing fax machines and personal computers are good examples of the problem. Xerox was committed to identifying breakthrough technologies, but was unable to grasp the opportunities it had in other areas. Executive demands for predictability killed both projects.[184] Too many managers demand data and clarity when they should be listening and helping people accomplish what they believe they can do.

Additional trouble and work

Change always creates additional trouble and work. We have to do the work we've always done and we also have to do the additional work necessary to change what we've always done. The effort takes more time at exactly the moment most of us already feel pressured. Many of us unfortunately simply decide the effort isn't worth it.

Politics and structure

We have all developed habits and routines that enable us to get work done. During periods of transition, familiar and predictable relationships give way to new associations and new techniques. Change forces us to re-examine past practices and redesign systems and procedures with which we have been comfortable. These issues raise all kinds of questions about the politics and structure of any organization.

Each of these blocks to new ideas is real. Because we are being pressured to create the future while we manage the present, it isn't surprising that we frequently get caught up in the forces of the whirlwind and lose our sense of direction. Ken Olsen, the former chairman of Digital Equipment Corporation (DEC), exemplified this problem by misunderstanding the importance of personal computers, open systems, and reduced instruction set computing during the 1980s.[185] Edson DeCastro, former chairman of Data General, stated that his "biggest mistake was failing to get Data General into the PC business. Few companies are able to participate in the next wave of technology because they are blinded by the business at hand."[186] Assessing how various issues might affect us and overcoming these blocks to new ideas becomes increasingly important if we are to create a better future.

■ MOVING TO A DIFFERENT FUTURE

> "The journey of a thousand miles begins with the first step."
> — *Anonymous*

One of the challenges we face is to build a shared understanding of how we can manage and experience change. Our experience to date suggests there are criteria which have to be met if we are to manage change effectively.

An easier way

We embrace changes that make life easier rather than harder. Early computer programs that ballyhooed computerizing recipes and telephone numbers were more trouble than they were worth. The development of spreadsheet, database and word processing programs represented a breakthrough because they enabled us to accomplish what we wanted to do more easily than would have been otherwise possible. Consolidated monthly statements from brokerage firms help us keep track of our financial transactions. Air casts for broken bones are easier to use because, unlike older plaster casts, they can be removed. For people who don't like to get out of bed in the morning, the timer on the coffee pot makes mornings bearable. None of us accepts changes that make our lives more difficult, but most of us at least try to implement changes that make our lives easier.

Simplicity

Change is more easily accepted if it holds the promise of making life simpler rather than more complex. Many of us still have trouble with video tape machines and microwave ovens, while innovations in photography, such as automatic focus, light adjustment and timers, are a good example of the value of simplicity and have enabled millions of us to take better pictures.

On a broader level, simplifying management systems by organizing around functions rather than departments usually results in simpler systems with fewer meetings, less paperwork and people gaining a sense of pride and control over their work. Such innovations whether in products or in systems gain wide acceptance — complexity doesn't.

Ease of transition

The easier it is to make the changes being proposed, the more likely we are to be willing to undertake them. The automotive and energy fields are examples of areas in which change is especially difficult; because the transition we need to make is both far reaching and expensive. Redesigning automotive production systems means changes in production lines, supplier systems and neighborhood gas stations. Using solar energy still requires us to alter residential and commercial heating and cooling systems. The ease with which we can set aside the old while we pick up the new is a major consideration in how rapidly new ideas are accepted.

Small steps

At one time or another, we have all faced the difficulties inherent in undertaking massive change or big projects. These projects are always more manageable when we break them down into smaller parts. Almost every business at one time or another stumbles because of a preoccupation with grand design rather than the incremental steps required for success. Focusing on small steps is a key to progress and change. Success, paradoxically, comes both from grand designs and the small steps we can take to get there.

Words and symbols

Using familiar ideas and words helps each of us gain a better understanding of change and what we need to do. Frequently professionals feel the need to coin new 50-cent words when the more familiar would be clearer and more useful — "fifth generation computers" is a harder idea to grasp than "building machines that think like people."

Flexibility

Flexibility is a key to gaining acceptance for new ideas. In the industrial society, we sought perfect solutions to complex issues. Gaining acceptance for new ideas requires much greater flexibility. Murphy's Law tells us that everything that can possibly go wrong will. As a result, our original ideas will invariably change. Steven Jobs and Stephen Wozniak started out with the idea of making computer boards. They built the first Apple I Computer in response to a customer's request. Their flexibility enabled them to build the Apple II and the rest, as they say, is history.

Costs

The cost of proposed innovations has to either be worth the time, trouble, energy and money they require, or lower than the cost of the present way we do things. Changes that require more time, trouble, energy and money on an ongoing basis aren't worth it. My WordPerfect, Lotus 1-2-3, and Harvard Graphics programs are worth more than their cost and the time they took to learn because I've saved thousands of hours of work.

■ A FINAL STORY

There is a wonderful story that captures the spirit of our present situation. Years ago, the people of a small town periodically faced problems and challenges. Each time there were difficulties, the town's leaders would seek guidance from a wise old man who lived alone in a cave above the town. He would advise them on what they should do and his advice was invariably helpful. Not surprisingly, the town's leaders came to believe the old man knew all there was to know. Eventually, there came a day when a teenage boy decided he would prove that the old man could not be as wise as the leaders thought. He would ask a question that could not be answered. The boy's plan was to go to the old man with a live bird in his hand and ask whether the bird was alive or dead. If the old man said the bird was alive, the boy would crush it. If the old man said the bird was dead, the boy would open his hand and let it fly. The boy went up the mountain to the cave and asked the old man the question. The old man thought for a while and then responded, "It all depends on you."

That story summarizes where each of us is today. The changes and challenges we face are not abstractions, but realities that touch each of us every day. The future won't just happen — it will be shaped by what each of us does today, tomorrow, next week, next month and next year. It is a time of extraordinary opportunity. The question is: what will each of us decide to do?

ENDNOTES

1   Daniel J. Boorstin, *The Discoverers: A History of Man's Search To Know His World and Himself,* A Personal Note to the Reader Section, Vintage Books — A Division of Random House, New York, NY, 1983, p. XVI.

2   John Kenneth Galbraith, *The Affluent Society — The Economics of the Age of Opulence,* Houghton Mifflin Publishers, Boston, 1958.

3   Ellen Neuborne, "Home Depot Scores With Service," *USA Today,* July 23, 1992, p. B1.

4   Personal conversation with Tom Jorgens.

5   Ruth Simon with Graham Button, "What I Learned in the '80s," *Forbes,* Jan. 8, 1990, p. 114.

6   TRW Advertisement, 1989.

7   Diane D'Amico, Ethic Workshop—"Doctoral Dropout Encourages Teachers," *The Press of Atlantic City,* N.J., Nov. 22, 1990, p. D1.

8   Virgil Berry, Analyst at A.T. Kearney, *Fortune,* Jan. 14, 1991, p. 31.

9   Dun & Bradstreet Software Ad in *Forbes,* 1992.

10 Personal conversation with Jeffrey Hallett, president, Present Futures Group in Washington, D.C.

11 Paul Hawken, The New Economy, Introduction and Chapter 1 — The Decline of the Mass Economy, Halt Reinhart Wilson. New York, 1983. See also Peter F. Drucker, Management and the World's Work, *Harvard Business Review,* Sept./Oct. 1988, p. 65 ff.

12 Manhattan, *Inc. Magazine,* Cash Register Column, 1990, p. 122.

13 Gretchen Morgenson, "The Buyout That Saved Safeway," *Forbes* Nov. 12, 1990, p. 88 ff.

14 Acura Advertisement, *New Yorker Magazine,* May 9, 1992.

15 Toni Mack, "Energizing A Bureaucracy," *Forbes,* Sept. 17, 1990, p. 76 ff.

16 Maggie McComas, "Cutting Costs Without Killing the Business," *Fortune,* Oct. 13, 1986, p. 70.

17 Digital Equipment Ad in *Forbes Magazine,* June 25, 1990.

18 John F. Welch Jr., "We've Got To Simplify and Delegate More," Today's Leaders Look To Tomorrow, Ideas for the 1990s, *Fortune,* March 26, 1990, p. 30. See also Noel M. Tichy and Stratford Sherman, *Control Your Destiny or Someone Else Will,* Currency Doubleday, New York, 1993.

19 Walter Wriston, "The Refrigerator's Revolutionary Role," Today's Leaders Look To Tomorrow, Ideas for the 1990s, *Fortune,* March 26, 1990, p. 64.

20 Personal interview with Charles McCall, HBO & Company of Atlanta, Ga.

21 Histoire - d'UnCrime, Part 5, Section 10, 1851-1852.

22 Frank Rose, "A New Age for Business?," *Fortune,* Oct. 8, 1990, p. 162.

23 ibid.

[24] Ann B. Fisher, "The New Debate Over the Very Rich," *Fortune*, June 29, 1992, p. 42.

[25] Nancy Miller, "Realtors are Upbeat in New Orleans," *USA Today*, Nov. 9, 1990, p. B1.

[26] For example, see Timothy Ferris, *The Mind's Sky*, Bantom Books, New York, N.Y., Feb. 1992.

[27] Daniel Boorstin, *The Americans: The Democratic Experience*, Vintage Books — A Division of Random House Publishing, New York, Aug. 1974, p. 357.

[28] Steven Prokesch, "Many Are Adopting A New Creed That Puts Corporate Survival Above All Else. The Results: A Generation of Ruthless Management," *The New York Times*, Jan. 25, 1987, Section II, p. 17.

[29] Staff Writer, "A Special News Report On People And Their Jobs In Offices, Fields and Factories," Labor Letter Section, *Wall Street Journal*, June 19, 1990, p. 1.

[30] *Webster's Ninth New Collegiate Dictionary*, Merriam Webster, 1986, p. 1211.

[31] John Markoff, "Future of Big Computing: A Triumph for Lilliputians," *The New York Times*, Nov. 25, 1990, p. 11.

[32] Andrew Hodges, Alan Turing, *The Enigma*, Touchstone Books by Simon & Schuster, New York, 1983.

[33] Heinz R. Pagels, *The Dreams of Reason*, Bantam Books, New York, 1988, preface p. 13.

[34] Sharon Begley with Daniel Glick, "The Handwriting of God," *Newsweek*, May 4, 1992, p. 76.

[35] George F. Will, *Men At Work — The Craft of Baseball*, Chapter 1 - "The Manager — Tony La Russa — On the Edge," Macmillan Publishing Co., New York, 1990, p. 7-75.

[36] Bernie Ward, "Drivers, Start Your Computers!," Technology Section in *SKY Magazine*, April 1990, p. 90 ff.

[37] The Healthcare Forum, Executive Education Series Cover, Feb., 1992.

[38] Michael Lewis, *Liar's Poker*, the Penguin Group, Viking Penguin, a division of Penguin Books, USA, Inc. New York, 1989, p. 134 ff.

[39] Rollin Pampel, CNN Interview, June 14, 1990.

[40] Jerry Adler, "Communicating Bit by Bit," *Newsweek*, May 21, 1990, p. 74 f.

[41] John Markoff, "Tiny Disks for Tiny Computer," Tech Notes Column, *The New York Times*, April 5, 1992, p. F7.

[42] Marshall Ledger, "Electronics in the Body Shop," John Hopkins Alumni Consortium, Aug. 1988, page I ff.

[43] Edmund L. Andrews, "Sensing the Presence of Potential Problems," *The New York Times*, May 6, 1990, p. F9.

[44] "Computers to Speed Shipping," Tomorrow in Brief Column, *The Futurist*, Jan./Feb. 1987, p. 3.

[45] Clare Ansberry, "Steel Industry Is On the Verge of David and Goliath Test," *Wall Street Journal*, Oct. 17, 1989, p. 10A.

[46] Otis Port, "Creating Chips an Atom at a Time," *Business Week*, July 29, 1991, p. 54.

[47] Evert Clark, "America Can Beat Anyone in High Tech, Just Ask Bruce Merrifield," Science & Technology Section, *Business Week*, April 7, 1986, p. 94.

[48] William E. Sheeline, "Who Needs the Stock Exchange?," *Fortune*, Nov. 19, 1990, p. 119 ff.

[49] ibid.

[50] Evert Clark, "America Can Beat Anyone in High Tech, Just Ask Bruce Merrifield," Science & Technology Section, *Business Week*, April 7, 1986, p. 94.

[51] Melinda Beck, et. al., "The Doctor's Suicide Van," Society-Aging Section, *Newsweek*, June 18, 1990, p. 46 ff.

[52] Alvin Toffler, *PowerShift: Knowledge, Wealth and Violence At The Edge of The 21st Century*, Bantam Books, New York, 1990, p. 102 ff.

[53] John Hillkirk and Paul Hoversten, "Devastating AT&T Outrage May Be Omen," *USA Today*, Jan. 17, 1990, p. 1A.

[54] Emily Card, "Credit Rating," *The Consumer Reports Money Book*, Consumer Report Books, Consumers Union of the United States, 1992, p. 125-126.

[55] From the L.L. Bean Manual - "The Golden Rule"

[56] Staff Writer, "The Year of the Brand," *The Economist*, Dec. 12, 1988, p. 95 ff.

[57] IBM Advertisement, *Forbes*, Sept. 8, 1991, p. 74F.

[58] Peter H. Lewis, "In A Turnabout, I.B.M. Says, 'We'll Talk to Anybody,'" The Executive Computer Section, *The New York Times*, March 22, 1992, p. 8F.

[59] "King Customer," *Business Week*, March 12, 1990, pp. 88-90.

[60] This has generally been attributed to Henry Ford although there does not exist an adequate source for it.

[61] Xerox Advertisement, *Wall Street Journal*, Sept. 7, 1990, p. C18.

[62] Walter Roessing, "Big League Edibles," *SKY Magazine*, July 1990, pp. 54-61.

[63] Wayne Burkan, Presentation to Goodhue County National Bank Retreat, Red Wing, Minn., Sept. 13, 1989.

[64] Tom Atchison Presentation to the Baptist Health System in Knoxville, Tenn., Feb. 5, 1992.

[65] Peter Steinfels, "For Catholic Charities, Caritas Mastercard," *The New York Times*, February 4, 1989, p. 16.

[66] Susan Lee, "What's With The Casino Society?" *Forbes*, Sept. 22, 1986, p. 151.

[67] Doug Podolsky, "Big claims no proof," *U.S. News & World Report*, Sept. 23, 1991, p. 77.

[68] David Manasian, "British Banks Abandon Standoffish Ways," *Wall Street Journal*, Feb. 28, 1989, p. A14.

[69] Theodore Levitt, *The Marketing Imagination*, The Free Press, A Division of Macmillan, Inc., New York, 1983, 1986, p. 72.

[70] Jan Carlzon, *Moments of Truth*, Harper and Row Publishing, New York, 1987.

[71] Paul B. Brown, "The Real Cost of Customer Service," *INC Magazine*, Sept. 1990, p. 49.

[72] Staff Writer, "Selling Is Believing," Hands On Section, *INC Magazine*, July 1990, p. 95.

[73] Personal conversation with Don Beveredge of Beveredge Business Systems, Barrington, Ill., June 1991.

[74] Don Beveredge, *The Yes Syndrome*, Beveredge Business Systems, Barrington, Ill., 1982.

[75] Joe Bernard, freelance writer, Genius Column, *TWA Ambassador Magazine*, April 1991, p. 38.

[76] Patricia Sellers, "Getting Customers To Love You," *Fortune*, March 13, 1989, p. 38 ff.

[77] Robert L. Desatnick, *Managing To Keep The Customer, The Silent Majority Chart*, Jossey-Bass Publishers, Inc., San Francisco, Calif., 1987.

[78] Joan C. Szabo, "Service=Survival," *Nations Business*, March 1989, p. 16 ff.

[79] James Traub, "Into the Mouths of Babes," *The New York Times Magazine*, July 24, 1988, p. 18 ff.

[80] American Survey, "Voter's Revenge," *The Economist*, Nov. 19, 1988, p. 33.

[81] Haya El Nasser, "Cities take stand on Cabbies: Be Nice!," *USA Today*, April 30, 1990, p. A1.

[82] Diane Thormodsgard Presentation to Lutheran Social Services, Oct. 28-29, 1988.

[83] Daniel J. Boorstin, *The Americans: The Democratic Experience*, Vintage Books - A Division of Random House, New York, 1973, p. 97.

[84] Patricia Sellers, "Getting Customers To Love You," *Fortune*, March 13, 1989, p. 39.

[85] Conversation with Dean Paulus, Kent Garwin of 3M Corporation, Oct. 19, 1990.

[86] Robert Kaufmann, "Report from the Headmaster," Publication of Deerfield Academy, Spring 1991, p. 3.

[87] Ernest L. Boyer, "For Education: National Strategy, Local Control," *The New York Times*, Nov. 26, 1989.

[88] Jay Finegan, "Are Bigger Banks Bad for Small Business," *INC Magazine*, Dec. 1987, p 161.

[89] Personal observations of real estate agents in working sessions over the last 10 years.

[90] Daniel J. Boorstin, *The Americans: The Democratic Experience*, Vintage Books, New York, Aug. 1974, pp. 340-341.

[91] George Reedy, *The Presidency in Flux*, Columbia University Press, New York, 1973, p. 11-16.

[92] Claudia H. Deutsch, NYT Writer, "Manville's Chief Exec Devises Cure for 'CEO Disease'," the *Denver Post*, Dec. 22, 1991, p. 31.

[93] Carol J. Loomis, "We're Eager to Put on a New Set of Armor and Do Battle ... the Helmet is Dented," *Fortune*, July 15, 1991, p. 42.

[94] Manhattan, *Inc. Magazine*, Cash Register Column, 1990, p. 122.

[95] Peter F. Drucker, "The Coming of the New Organization," *Harvard Business Review*, Jan./Feb. 1988, pp. 45-53.

[96] Joe Bernard, Genius Section, *TWA Ambassador Magazine*, April 1991, pp. 38-42.

[97] Private Conversation, Harold DeNeal, retired employee, National Steel Company, April 21, 1991.

[98] John D. McDonald, *Cancel All Our Vows*, Random House/Fawcett Books, New York, 1953, 1985, p. 15.

[99] Toni Mack, "Energizing A Bureaucracy," *Forbes*, Sept. 17, 1990, p. 76.

[100] Personal conversation with Robert C. Hanna.

[101] W. Edwards Deming, *Out of The Crisis*, Massachusetts Institute of Technology, Center for Advanced Engineering Study, Cambridge, Mass., 1982, 1986, pp. 167-182.

[102] J.M. Juran, *Juran on Planning for Quality*, The Free Press - A Division of Macmillan, Inc., New York, 1988, p. 5.

[103] W. Edwards Deming, *Out of the Crisis*, Massachusetts Institute of Technology, Center for Advanced Engineering Study, Cambridge, Mass., 1982.

[104] Conversation with Dean Paulus, Kent Garwin, 3M Corporation, Oct. 19, 1990.

[105] Stuart Kaminsky, *Murder on the Yellow Brick Road*, Penguin Books, New York, 1977, p. 121.

[106] Jeff DeWar, QCI International, Quality Chart.

[107] Elisa Tinsley, "Bank Gets $2M Lesson," *USA Today*, Feb. 21, 1989, p. 1A.

[108] "Jack Welch's Lessons for Success," Managing/Book Excerpt, *Fortune*, Jan. 25, 1993, p. 86 ff. See also, Ruth Simon with Graham Button, "What I Learned in the Eighties," *Forbes*, Jan. 8, 1990, p. 100.

[109] Rosabeth Moss Kanter, *The Change Masters*, Simon and Schuster, New York, 1983, p. 69 ff.

[110] James Sterngold, *Burning Down the House: How Greed, Deceit, and Bitter Revenge Destroyed E.F. Hutton*, Summit Books, New York, 1990.

[111] Robert L. Desatnick, *Managing To Keep The Customer, The Silent Majority Chart*, p. 3, Jossey-Bass Publishers, San Francisco, 1987.

[112] Phil Patton, "Reshaping Ford's Future," *Vis a Vis Magazine*, Oct. 1987 p. 94.

[113] "Smart Designs — Quality Is The New Style," *Business Week*, April 11, 1988, p. 102-108.

[114] Joel Dreyfuss, "Victories In The Quality Crusade," *Fortune*, Oct. 10, 1988, pp. 80-88.

[115] William Schuman Interview, National Public Radio, Feb. 17, 1992.

[116] Perry Pascarella, "The Amazing Thing About Quality," *Industrial Week*, Sept. 7, 1989, p. 7.

[117] John Donne (1573-1631), *Devotions Upon Emergent Occasions*, Meditations No. 6, 1624.

[118] Harold L. Hodgkinson, *The Same Client: The Demographics of Education and Service Delivery Systems*, IEL Institute for Educational Leadership, Inc. and Center for Demographics Policy, Washington, D.C., Sept. 1989.

[119] MGMA, *Cost Survey: 1992 Report Based on 1991 Data*, Medical Group Management Association, Englewood, Colo., Aug. 1992, and NAR, *Real Estate Brokerage Income, Expenses, Profits 1991*, Real Estate Business Series.

[120] Peter E. Drucker on the cover of the American Management Association, Catalog of Seminars, Aug. 1990-April 1991.

[121] Conversation with Scott Jones, president, Goodhue County National Bank, Red Wing, Minn.

[122] Claudia H. Deutsch, "Colgate's Next Trick: Controlling the Chaos," *The New York Times*, Aug. 6, 1989, Section 3, p. E6.

[123] Udayan Gupta, "How Big Companies Are Joining Forces With Little Ones For Mutual Advantages," *Wall Street Journal*, Feb. 25, 1991, p. B1.

[124] Brenton R. Schlender, "Apple's Japanese Ally," *Fortune*, Nov. 4, 1991, p. 151.

[125] Marcus W. Brauchli and Masayoshi Kanabayashi, "Japanese Banks Face Sharper Competition, Industry Consolidation," *Wall Street Journal*, May 30, 1990, p. A1.

[126] "Money Clip" section, *U.S. News & World Report*, Aug. 26/Sept. 2, 1993, p. 18.

[127] J. Daniel Beckum, "Making A Community Agenda," *Healthcare Forum Journal*, Jan./Feb. 1992, p. 41.

[128] John Markoff, "Armistice for Apple and Microsoft," *The New York Times*, July 16, 1992, p. C1.

[129] Wilton Woods, "The U.S. Must Do as GM Has Done," *Fortune*, Feb. 13, 1989, p. 70 ff.

[130] Bryan Burrough and John Helyar, *Barbarians At The Gate*, Harper and Row Publishers, New York, 1990.

[131] Scott McMurray and Jeffrey Taylor, "Rivalry Hinders Any Attempt to Unify Two Chicago Exchanges," *Wall Street Journal*, Sept. 26, 1990, p. C1 and C8.

[132] Matt Roush, "Risk-Taking TV's Noble Failure, Qualified Success, But Most Plough Middle Ground," Life Section, *USA Today*, Dec. 12, 1990, p. 1D.

[133] Barnaby J. Feder, "The 'Pharmers' Who Breed Cows That Can Make Drugs," Technology Column, *The New York Times*, Feb. 9, 1992, p. D3.

[134] Daniel Yergin, *The Prize: The Epic Quest for Oil, Money & Power*, Simon & Schuster, New York, 1991, p. 13.

[135] Peter Schwartz, *The Art of the Long View*, Doubleday, a division of Bantam Doubleday Dell Publishing Group, Inc. New York, 1991, p. 59.

[136] Fred Moody, "Mr. Software," *The New York Times Magazine*, Aug. 25, 1991, p. 28.

[137] Peter Coy, "AT&T Reaches Out and Taps Some New Talent," Information Processing Column, *Business Week*, July 2, 1991, p. 80.

[138] Susan Moffat, "Japan's New Personalized Production," *Fortune*, Oct, 22, 1990, p. 132 ff.

[139] Joel Kurtzman, Business Diary Column, *The New York Times*, Aug. 18, 1991, p. F2.

[140] Joseph T. Plummer, "Changing Values," *The Futurist*, Jan./Feb. 1989, p. 8-13.

[141] Thomas S. Kuhn, *The Structure of Scientific Revolution*, University of Chicago Press, Chicago, Ill., 1962, 1970, p. 109.

[142] ibid.

[143] ibid, p. 45-51.

[144] John Kenneth Galbraith, Reprinted in *Johns Hopkins University Alumni Magazine*, Summer 1988, Vol. 88, No. 2.

[145] Wayne Burkan Presentation at the Goodhue Financial Services Board Retreat, Red Wing, Minnesota on Sept. 13, 1989.

[146] Lester C. Thurow, *Dangerous Currents: The State of Economics*, Random House Publishing, New York, 1983, Introduction p. XIII-XIX.

[147] ibid, p. 237.

[148] Thomas S. Kuhn, *The Structure of Scientific Revolution*, University of Chicago Press, Chicago, Ill., 1970, p. 109. For an additional discussion of this same

issue of confusion about the meanings of words see William Lutz, *Doublespeak*, Harper and Row Publishing, New York, 1989.

[149] Marvin Harris, *America Now*, Touchstone Books through Simon and Schuster, New York, 1981, p. 18.

[150] James Traub, "Into the Mouths of Babes," *The New York Times Magazine*, July 24, 1988, p. 18 ff.

[151] "Air Ministries: Unequal Time" Chart, p. 8, Vital Statistics, *Newsweek*, April 9, 1990.

[152] The Associated Press, "98% of audited hospital bills wrong," *The Denver Post*, Nov. 10, 1988, p. 15A.

[153] Erik Calonius, "The FAA's Loose Grip On Air Safety," *Fortune*, Oct. 8, 1990, p. 85 ff.

[154] 'One Line On The News' column, *USA Today*, Aug. 3, 1988.

[155] Nancy Traver, "The Housing Hustle," Nation Section, *TIME Magazine*, June 26, 1989, p. 18 ff.

[156] Timothy Noah, "The Next Budget Shell Game," *Newsweek*, Jan. 12, 1987, p. 22 ff.

[157] Barry Goldwater, 'Quote of the Day' Section, *USA Today*, Aug. 25, 1986.

[158] Ernest L. Boyer, *College: The Undergraduate Experience in America*, The Carnegie Foundation for the Advancement of Teaching, New York, 1987, Prologue, p. 2.

[159] Thomas J. Peters and Robert H. Waterman Jr., *In Search of Excellence*, Warner Books in cooperation with Harper and Row Publishers, New York, 1982, p. 119. This is from an Executive at Cadbury's.

[160] K.C. Cole, A Theory of Everything, *New York Times Magazine*, Oct. 18, 1987, p. 20 ff.

[161] Joel Barker, Paradigm Summary Notes, Infinity Limited, Inc., St. Paul, Minn., 1989.

[162] Dr. Niles Eldredge, *Time Frames*, Simon & Schuster, Inc., New York, 1985, p. 15. (Theory developed in 1972 with Stephen J. Gould.)

[163] Richard Foster, *Innovation: The Attacker's Advantage*, Summit Books, New York, 1986.

[164] Greyhound Ad with John Teets, Forbes, Sept. 25, 1989.

[165] Under the Gun, Other Comments Column, *Forbes*, March 5, 1990, p. 24.

[166] Jeremy Rifkin, *Time Frames — The Primary Conflict in Human History*, Henry Holt and Company, New York, 1987, p. 177.

[167] René Descartes Discourse on Methods and the Meditations Translated by F.E. Sutchiffe, Penguin Books, Ltd., Middlesex, England, 1968., p. 21.

[168] Martha T. Moore, "McDonald's Trashes Sandwich Boxes," *USA Today*, Nov. 2, 1990, p. 9B.

[169] John Donne (1573-1631), *Devotions Upon Emergent Occasions*, Meditations XVII, 1624.

[170] Charles C. Mann, "The Man With All The Answers," *The Atlantic Monthly*, Jan. 1990, p. 45 ff.

[171] AP Story, "Atwater says He's Sorry for Remark on Dukasis," *The Denver Post*, Jan. 31, 1991, p. 17A.

[172] Sylvia Nasas, "The Outrage Index Rises: Wall Street Feels the Heat," *New York Times*, Sept. 22, 1991, p. 4E.

[173] Phyllis Therous, "Use It or Lose It," *The New York Times Book Review*, Aug. 16, 1992, p. 25, on Thomas Moore, Care of the Soul.

[174] Phillip Heyman Ames, "Failing the Ethics Test," *Harvard Magazine*, Jan./Feb. 1992, p. 52.

[175] Sharon Shaw Johnson, "The Fix: Payoff for the House's Parking Tickets," *USA Today*, Oct. 9, 1991, p. 54.

[176] AP Story, "Milli Vanilli could lose Grammy," *Rocky Mountain News*, 1990, p. 73.

[177] John Acoda, "The Body Shop Owner Peddles Social Change," *Rocky Mountain News*, Nov. 19, 1992, p. 61.

[178] Jonathon Swift, "Thoughts on Various Subjects, Miscellanies, 1711.

[179] Allan Cox, "Focus on Teamwork, Vision and Values," *New York Times*, February 26, 1989. See also J. William Pfeiffer, Leonard D. Goodstein & Timothy M. Nolan, *Shaping Strategic Planning* Figure 2-4 p. 22, The Johnson & Johnson Credo, Pfeiffer & Company, San Diego, Calif.

[180] Joshua Levine, "An escalator? In Brooks Brothers," *Forbes*, July 9, 1990, p. 76 ff.

[181] ibid.

[182] AP Story, "Husband Testifies He Doesn't Want Embryos Destroyed," *Star Tribune*, Tenn., Aug. 9, 1989, p. 16A.

[183] Timothy McQuay and Jack Kelley, "Burial in Space Just Over the Horizon," *USA Today*, Sept. 9, 1986, p. 3A. And Staff Writer, Business Notes-Ventures Column, "Space Burial On Hold," *TIME Magazine*, Sept. 29, 1986, p. 59A.

[184] Douglas K. Smith and Robert C. Alexander, *Fumbling the Future*, William Morrow and Company, Inc., New York, 1988.

[185] Esther Dysson, "Re-Creating DEC," *Forbes*, March 30, 1992, p. 124.

[186] John R. Wilke, "Data General Board Ousts, Co-Founder," *Wall Street Journal*, Dec. 13, 1990, p. B1.

AN ASSESSMENT

APPENDIX

An Assessment

The changes discussed in *Managing the Whirlwind* mean we have to rethink how we arrange ourselves to accomplish our goals. When we step back from daily pressures and look at the changes occurring in the United States and around the world it's clear we have no choice but to change the way we manage our organizations. This appendix was designed to help us think about our present situations and assess our opportunities.

A grasp of reality

A grasp of reality is important in dealing with changes we will experience. This grasp of reality — at a minimum — involves the following questions.

	Not at all	Not very well	OK	Well	Very Well
I understand how the future could be different from the present:	.	.	.	.	.
• in my personal life	☐	☐	☐	☐	☐
• in my work	☐	☐	☐	☐	☐
I can list changes which could affect:	.	.	.	.	.
• my personal life	☐	☐	☐	☐	☐
• my work	☐	☐	☐	☐	☐
They include:	.	.	.	.	.
1. _____	.	.	.	.	.
2. _____	.	.	.	.	.
3. _____	.	.	.	.	.
I have a plan to manage those changes:	.	.	.	.	.
• in my personal life	☐	☐	☐	☐	☐
• in my work	☐	☐	☐	☐	☐
This plan means I will:	.	.	.	.	.
1. _____	.	.	.	.	.
2. _____	.	.	.	.	.
3. _____	.	.	.	.	.
4. _____	.	.	.	.	.

A grasp of reality (continued)	Not at all	Not very well	OK	Well	Very Well
My organization has demonstrated it can manage changes which could affect its future.	☐	☐	☐	☐	☐
My organization has demonstrated that it can manage the changes it anticipates.	☐	☐	☐	☐	☐

Actions I/we could take to improve:
I can take the following steps to do a better job of managing change.

1. _____
2. _____
3. _____
4. _____

Values

Every organization operates in accordance with values which shape the day-to-day behavior of people who work there. These values may be explicit and widely discussed, or implicit and tacitly understood, but every organization has them. Successful organizations have values that are explicit and widely understood; they shape everything it does. Whether their values relate to specific commitments such as how it treats people, its beliefs about integrity, or how it values innovation is less important than the fact that the organization stands for something and people know what it is.

Values can be thought of as characteristics we act on rather than possess. Some organizations have clearly defined the values that shape their behavior. Findley Adhesives in Milwaukee has a set of values bases on the idea that "Findley is committed to success by thinking, feeling and acting in the interests of its customers, employees and the communities in which we operate." Memorial Healthcare System in Houston has a Statement of Purpose and Values which defines its purpose, beliefs and the relationships it believes are important to carry out its mission. The idea that "business is business" and not related to values is giving way to the idea that organizations — like people — should embody values that shape their behavior.

Values (continued)

	Not at all	Not very well	OK	Well	Very Well
My organization has a clear statement of values.	☐	☐	☐	☐	☐
In my organization, we understand what those values mean and talk about them on an ongoing basis.	☐	☐	☐	☐	☐
Our customers know what we stand for.	☐	☐	☐	☐	☐
The people with whom we work know what we stand for.	☐	☐	☐	☐	☐

Actions I/we could take to improve:

I can take the following steps to do a better job ensuring that my colleagues and customers understand our values:

1. _____
2. _____
3. _____
4. _____

Vision

Whether they're called goals, a strategic plan or "visions for the future," successful people and organizations know where they are going. In the ideal, this sense of direction shapes personal decisions and, in an organization it shapes operating plans, budgets and hiring choices. Without a sense of direction, there is no criteria by which to measure success and no way to clarify what people should or should not do in their daily work.

I have a sense of what my personal life will be like:					
• next year..	☐	☐	☐	☐	☐
• in three years	☐	☐	☐	☐	☐
• in five years..	☐	☐	☐	☐	☐
• in 10 years	☐	☐	☐	☐	☐
I have a sense of how the work I do will be different:					
• next year..	☐	☐	☐	☐	☐
• in three years	☐	☐	☐	☐	☐
• in five years..	☐	☐	☐	☐	☐
• in 10 years	☐	☐	☐	☐	☐

	Not at all	Not very well	OK	Well	Very Well

Vision (continued)

My co-workers and I have a shared sense of
what we will be doing:
- next year .... ☐ ☐ ☐ ☐ ☐
- in three years .... ☐ ☐ ☐ ☐ ☐
- in five years... ☐ ☐ ☐ ☐ ☐
- in 10 years .... ☐ ☐ ☐ ☐ ☐

My organization has a clear vision of the future. .... ☐ ☐ ☐ ☐ ☐

I understand my organization's vision for the
future. .... ☐ ☐ ☐ ☐ ☐

My organization's vision for the future is understood
throughout the organization. .... ☐ ☐ ☐ ☐ ☐

Actions I/we could take to improve:

I can take the following steps to do a better job of
clarifying my/our vision for the future:

1. _____
2. _____
3. _____
4. _____

Information

Because living in the information society is different than living in
the industrial society, we need to rethink issues related to our own
personal development as well as how organizations manage information.

I invest in my own learning. .... ☐ ☐ ☐ ☐ ☐

Actions I/we could take to improve:

I need to develop the following skills:

1. _____
2. _____
3. _____
4. _____

Information (continued)

	Not at all	Not very well	OK	Well	Very Well
Our organization has a commitment to invest in people. They provide ongoing training opportunities.	☐	☐	☐	☐	☐
I have the necessary information to do my job.	☐	☐	☐	☐	☐
Our organization:					
• has too much information	☐	☐	☐	☐	☐
• has too little information	☐	☐	☐	☐	☐
Our organization continuously simplifies the information systems we use.	☐	☐	☐	☐	☐
Our organization does a good job of getting the right information to the right people at the right time.	☐	☐	☐	☐	☐
Financial management: We have redesigned our financial systems so I have the information I need.	☐	☐	☐	☐	☐
We need fewer people in our organization than we did five years ago.	☐	☐	☐	☐	☐
We continue to reduce paperwork in our organization.	☐	☐	☐	☐	☐

Actions I/we could take to improve.

I can take the following steps to do a better job of managing information:

1. _____
2. _____
3. _____
4. _____

Technology

Technology — the way we do things — is changing rapidly. As a result, we need to change. The following points focus on how technology might affect us.

	Not at all	Not very well	OK	Well	Very Well

Technology (continued)

I have a sense of which technologies could affect us
in the future:
* in my own work .... ☐ ☐ ☐ ☐ ☐
* in my organization's future .... ☐ ☐ ☐ ☐ ☐

I have identified the following products/services we
could provide because of the new technologies:
1. _____
2. _____
3. _____
4. _____

I have identified products/services we may not
provide because of new technologies, including:
1. _____
2. _____
3. _____
4. _____

We manage the introduction of new technologies
effectively. .... ☐ ☐ ☐ ☐ ☐

Actions I/we could take to improve:

I can take the following steps to do a better job of
managing technological change:
1. _____
2. _____
3. _____
4. _____

Customer service

One challenge every organization faces is how to increase resources devoted to serving customers and managing the future. This means overhead costs need to go down. We have to find simpler ways to do work. Successful organizations are able to look beyond pressures generated by their own structures and focus instead on how to invest more time, people and money in serving their customers and building for the future. In these companies, the percentage of total costs devoted to overhead goes down, not up.

Customer service (continued)

	Not at all	Not very well	OK	Well	Very Well
I see customers on a regular basis.	☐	☐	☐	☐	☐
My organization continuously increases its investment in customer service.	☐	☐	☐	☐	☐
We have reduced the steps necessary to accomplish what customers and clients would like us to do.	☐	☐	☐	☐	☐
I have a sense of what my customers/clients will expect in the future. They expect:					
1._____					
2._____					
3._____					
4._____					
Our organization has an understanding of what our customers/clients will expect in the future.	☐	☐	☐	☐	☐

Actions I/we could take to improve:
I can take the following steps to do a better job of managing customer service:

1._____
2._____
3._____
4._____

Questions of scale

Discussions of questions of scale now have to give way to focusing on people we serve and how we can simplify the work we do to meet their needs.

	Not at all	Not very well	OK	Well	Very Well
In our organization, we are able to focus on the work to be done rather than on the structure and politics of the organization.	☐	☐	☐	☐	☐
We are continuously reducing the number of departments in our organization.	☐	☐	☐	☐	☐

Questions of scale (continued)	Not at all	Not very well	OK	Well	Very Well
We continuously reduce the number of levels of management in our organization.	☐	☐	☐	☐	☐

Actions I/we could take to improve:
I can take the following steps to do a better job in managing quality:

1. _____
2. _____
3. _____
4. _____

Quality

Successful organizations are obsessed with quality. They strive to "conform to customer expectations" and "do the appropriate thing correctly the first time." Accepting the idea of business as usual is a prescription for disaster.

	Not at all	Not very well	OK	Well	Very Well
I understand what quality means for my work and how I do it.	☐	☐	☐	☐	☐
I have been trained in the tools necessary to manage systems effectively.	☐	☐	☐	☐	☐
In my organization we work in teams to simplify and improve the systems we use.	☐	☐	☐	☐	☐
Senior management in my organization has a strong commitment to quality.	☐	☐	☐	☐	☐

Actions I/we could take to improve:
I can take the following steps to do a better job of managing quality:

1. _____
2. _____
3. _____
4. _____

Collaboration

Collaboration will be increasingly important and the challenge for each of us is how well we can work with others.

	Not at all	Not very well	OK	Well	Very Well
I believe collaboration will be increasingly important.	☐	☐	☐	☐	☐
I spend time in other parts of the organization.	☐	☐	☐	☐	☐
I spend time in training sessions with people from different parts of the organization.	☐	☐	☐	☐	☐

Actions I/we could take to improve:
I can take the following steps to do a better job of collaborating:

1. _____
2. _____
3. _____
4. _____

Planning

Successful organizations see planning as a way to set the organization's direction and learn more about how it works. Planning is an ongoing responsibility for everyone, not an annual experience for a few. The process gives the opportunity and discipline to step back from day-to-day pressures, think about the longer-term and learn more about the business.

	Not at all	Not very well	OK	Well	Very Well
We do a good job of planning in our organization.	☐	☐	☐	☐	☐

Actions I/we could take to improve:
I can take the following steps to do a better job of planning:

1. _____
2. _____
3. _____
4. _____

Meetings

We spend a significant amount of our lives in meetings and the question is how well we use that time.

	Not at all	Not very well	OK	Well	Very Well
We manage meetings effectively in our organization.	☐	☐	☐	☐	☐
There is time for "learning meetings" in the organization.	☐	☐	☐	☐	☐
Information meetings are effective.	☐	☐	☐	☐	☐
In our organization we reach decisions clearly and move on.	☐	☐	☐	☐	☐

Actions I/we could take to improve:

I can take the following steps to do a better job of managing meetings:

1. _____
2. _____
3. _____
4. _____

INDEX

N

O

P

■

BIBLIOGRAPHY

Ardrey, Robert, *A Social Contract*, Atheneum, New York, 1970.

Augros, Robert and Stancius, George, *The New Biology*, New Science Library/ Shambhala Publications, Inc., Boston, 1987.

Augustine, Norman R., *Augustine's Laws*, Viking Penguin, Inc., New York, 1986.

Aulette, Ken, *Greed and Glory On Wall Street*, Warner Books, New York, 1986.

Barber, William J., *A History of Economic Thought*, Penguin Books, Ltd., Middlesex, 1967.

Barker, Joel Arthur, *Discovering the Future: The Business of Paradigms*, I.L.I Press, St. Paul, 1985.

Bateson, Gregory, *Steps To an Ecology of Mind*, Ballantine Books, New York, 1972.

Batra, Dr. Ravi, *The Great Depression of 1990*, Simon and Schuster, Inc., New York, 1987.

Belasco, James A., *Teaching Elephants to Dance: Empowering Change in Your Organization*, Crown Publishers, 1990.

Bell, Daniel, *The Coming of Post-Industrial Society*, Basic Books, Inc., New York, 1973.

Bell, Daniel and Kristol, Irving, *The Crisis In Economic Theory*, Basic Books, Inc., New York, 1981.

Bennis, Warren and Nanus, Burt, *Leaders*, Harper & Row, New York, 1985.

Bennis, Warren, *Why Leaders Can't Lead*, Jossey-Bass Publishers, San Francisco, 1989.

Bennis, Warren, *On Becoming a Leader*, Addison-Wesley Publishing Company, 1989.

Berger, Peter L., *Invitation to Sociology: A Humanistic Perspective*, Anchor Books, Garden City, 1963.

Berman, Morris, *The Reenchantment of the World*, Bantam Books, Toronto, 1956.

Beveridge, D.W. Jr., *The Yes Syndrome*, D.W. Beveridge, Jr. and Associates, Barrington, 1982. Bloom, Allan, *The Closing of the American Mind*, Simon and Schuster, Inc., New York, 1987.

Boorstin, Daniel, *The Discoverers - A History of Man's Search to Know His Word and Himself*, Vintage Books, New York, 1985.

Boorstin, Daniel J., *Democracy and Its Discontents*, Vintage Books, New York, 1974.

Boorstin, Daniel J., *The Americans: The Democratic Experience*, Vintage Books, New York, 1974.

Botkin, James W. and Elmanjra, Mahdi and Malitza, Mircea, *No Limits To Learning*, Pergamon Press, Oxford, 1979.

Brown, Lester R., *State of the World*, W.W. Norton and Company, New York, 1990.

Bucholz, Todd G., *New Ideas From Dead Economists*, First Plume Printing, New York, 1990.

Burnam, Tom, *The Dictionary of Misinformation*, Thomas Y. Crowell Company, New York, 1975.

Burns, James MacGregor, *Uncommon Sense*, Harper & Row, New York, 1972.

Burns, James MacGregor, *Leadership*, Harper & Row, New York, 1978.

Burrough, Bryan and Helyar, John, *Barbarians At the Gate: The Fall of RJR Nabisco*, Harper & Row, New York, 1990.

Bynam, William C. Ph.D. with Cox, Jeff, *Zapp!*, Development Dimensions International Press, Pittsburgh, 1989.

Campbell, Joseph, *Myths To Live By*, Bantam Books, New York, 1978. Capra, Fritjof, *The Turning Point*, Bantam Books, Toronto, 1982.

Carlzon, Jan, *Moments of Truth*, Ballinger Publishing Company, New York, 1987.

Casti, John L., *Paradigms Lost*, William Morrow & Company, Inc., New York, 1989.

Celente, Gerald with Milton, Tom, *Trend Tracking*, John Wiley and Sons, New York, 1990.

Cerf, Christopher and Navasky, Victor, *The Experts Speak*, Pantheon Books, New York, 1984.

Cetron, Marvin and O'Toole, Thomas, *Encounters With the Future*, McGraw-Hill Book Company, New York, 1982.

Chandler, Alfred D. Jr., *Strategy and Struggle: Chapters In the History of the American Industrial Enterprise*, The M.I.T. Press, Cambridge, 1962.

Clifford, Donald J. Jr. and Cavanah, Richard E., *The Winning Performance*, Bantam Books, Toronto, 1985.

Cox, Harvey, *The Secular City*, The Macmillan Company, New York, 1966.

Crosby, Philip B., *Quality Is Free*, New American Library, New York, 1979.

Crosby, Philip B., *Quality Without Tears*, New American Library, New York, 1984.

Davis, Stanley M., *Future Perfect*, Addison-Wesley Publishing Company, Inc., Reading, 1987.

Deal, Terrence E. and Kennedy, Allan A., *Corporate Cultures*, Addison- Wesley Publishing Company, Reading, 1982.

Deming, W. Edward, *Out of the Crisis*, Massachusetts Institute of Technology, Center for Advanced Engineering Study, Cambridge, 1982.

DePree, Max, *Leadership Is An Art*, Doubleday, New York, 1989.

Descartes, Rene, *Discourse On Method and the Meditations*, Penguin Books, Ltd., Middlesex, 1968.

DeTocqueville, Alexis, *Democracy In America*, Vintage Books, New York, 1945.

Drucker, Peter F., *Innovation and Entrepreneurship*, Harper & Row, New York, 1985.

Drucker, Peter F., *The Future of* Industrial Man, The New American Library of World Literature, Inc., New York, 1970.

Drucker, Peter F., *The Practice of Management*, Harper & Row, New York, 1954.

Drucker, Peter F., *The New Realities*, Harper & Row, New York, 1989.

Eldredge, Niles, *Times Frames*, Simon and Schuster, Inc., New York, 1985.

Feigenaum, Edward A. and McCorduck, Pamela, *The Fifth Generation*, Addison-Wesley Publishing Company, Reading, 1983.

Ferguson, Marilyn, *The Aquarian Conspiracy*, J.P. Tarcher, Inc., Los Angeles, 1980.

Ferris, Timothy, *Coming of Age In the Milky Way*, William Morrow and Company, Inc., New York, 1988.

Ferris, Timothy, *The Mind's Sky*, Bantom Books, New York, 1992. ,

Feynman, Richard P., *"Surely You're Joking, Mr. Feynman!"*, Bantam Books, Toronto, 1985.

Ford, Julienne, *Paradigms and Fairy Tales*, Routledge & Kegan Paul, London, 1975.

Foster, Richard, *Innovation: The Attacker's Advantage*, Summit Books, New York, 1986.

Fox, Stephen, *The Mirror Makers*, Vintage Books, New York, 1984.

Galbraith, John Kenneth, *The Affluent Society*, Houghton Mifflin Company, Boston, 1958.

Gardner, John W., *Excellence*, Harper & Row, New York, 1961.

Garreau, Joel, *The Nine Nations of North America*, Houghton Mifflin Company, Boston, 1981.

Giamatti, A. Bartlett, *Take Time for Paradise: Americans and their Games*, Summit Books, 1989.

Ginzberg, Eli and Vojta, George, *Beyond Human Scale*, Basic Books, Inc., New York, 1985.

Gitlow, Howard S. and Shelly J. Gitlow, *The Deming Guide to Quality and Competitive Position*, Prentice-Hall Inc, (a division of Simon & Schuster) Englewood Cliffs, New Jersey, 1987.

Gleick, James, *Chaos*, Viking Penguin Inc., New York, 1987.

Goldratt, Eliyaha M. and Cox, Jeff, *The Goal: A Process of Ongoing Improvement*, North River Press, Inc., Croton-on-Hudson, 1986.

Gould, Stephen Jay, *An Urchin In the Storm*, W.W. Norton & Company, New York, 1987.

Gribbon, John, *In Search of Schrodinger's Cat*, Bantam Books, Toronto, 1984.

Guaspari, John, *I Know It When I See It*, ACACOM, New York, 1985.

Hallett, Jeffrey J., *Worklife Visions: Redefining Work for the Information Economy*, American Society for Personnel Administration, Alexandria, Virginia, 1987.

Handy, Charles, *The Age of Unreason*, Harvard Business School Press, Boston, MA. 1990.

Harris, Marvin, *America Now*, Simon and Schuster, Inc., New York, 1981.

Hawken, Paul, *Growing A Business*, Fireside Books, Simon and Schuster, Inc., New York City, New York, 1987.

Hawkings, Stephen W., *A Brief History of Time*, Bantam Books, Toronto, 1988.

Heider, John, *The Tao of Leadership*, Bantam Books, Toronto, 1985.

Heymann, Tom, *On An Average Day*, Ballantine, New York, 1989.

Hirsch, E.D. Jr., Kett, Joseph F. and Trefil, James, *The Dictionary of Cultural Literacy: What Every American Needs To Know*, Houghton Mifflin, Boston, 1988.

Hodges, Andrew, *Alan Turing: The Enigma*, Simon and Schuster, Inc., New York, 1983.

Hodgson, Godfrey, *America In Our Time*, Vintage Books, New York, 1976.

Hofstadter, Richard, *Social Darwinism in American Thought*, Beacon Press, Boston, 1955.

Juran, J.M., *Juran on Planning for Quality*, The Free Press, New York, 1988.

Kaminsky, Stuart, *Murder on the Yellow Brick Road*, Penguin Books, New York, 1977.

Kanter, Rosabeth Moss, *The Change Masters*, Simon and Schuster, Inc., New York, 1983.

Kanter, Rosabeth Moss, *When Giants Learn to Dance*, Simon & Schuster, 1989.

Kline, Morris, *Mathematics, The Loss of Certainty*, Oxford University Press, Oxford, 1980.

Kochan, Thomas A. and Katz, Harry C. and Mower, Nancy R., *Worker Participation and American Unions*, W.E. Upjohn Institute for Employment Research, Kalamazoo, 1984.

Kotter, John P., *The Leadership Factor*, The Free Press, New York, 1988.

Kriegel, Robert J. and Patler, Louis, *If it ain't broke...BREAK IT!* Warner Books, A Time Warner Inc. Company, New York, 1991.

Kuhn, Thomas S., *The Structure of Scientific Revolutions*, The University of Chicago Press, Chicago, 1970.

Kuhn, Thomas S., *The Essential Tension*, The University of Chicago Press, Chicago, 1979.

Levitt, Theodore, *The Marketing Imagination*, The Free Press, Macmillan, New York, 1983, 1986.

Lewis, Michael, *Liar's Poker*, Penguin Books, New York, 1989.

Lindaman, Edward B. and Lippitt, Ronald O., *Choosing the Future You Prefer*, Development Publications, Washington, 1979.

Louv, Richard, *America II*, Jeremy P. Tarcher, Inc., Los Angeles, 1983.

Lutz, William, *DoubleSpeak*, Harper & Row Publishers, New York, NY, 1989.

Martin, Albro, *Railroads Triumphant*, Oxford University Press, New York, 1992.

Mathein, J. Daniel and Squire, Morris B., *How To Make Decisions That Pay Off,* Pluribus Press, Chicago, 1982.

Miller, Douglas T. and Nowak, Marion, *The Fifties: The Way We Really Were,* Doubleday & Company, Inc., Garden City, 1977.

Miller, Lawrence M., *Barbarians To Bureaucrats,* Clarkson N. Potter, Inc., New York, 1989.

Miller, Lawrence M., *American Spirit,* William Morrow and Company, Inc., New York, 1984.

Morris, Richard, *Time's Arrows,* Simon and Schuster, Inc., New York, 1985.

Naisbitt, John, *Megatrends,* Warner Books, New York, 1982, 1984.

O'Rourke, P.J., *Parliament of Whores - A Lone Humorist Attempts to Explain the Entire US Government,* A Morgan Entrekin Book, The Atlantic Monthly Press, New York, 1991.

Ohmae, Kenichi, *The Mind of the Strategist,* Penguin Books, Ltd., Middlesex, 1982.

Ouchi, William, *The M-Form Society,* Addison-Wesley Publishing Company, Reading, 1984.

Ouchi, William G., *Theory Z: How American Business Can Meet the Japanese Challenge,* Avon Books, Addison Wesley Publishing Company, New York City, New York, 1981.

Pagels, Heinz, *The Dreams of Reason,* Bantom Books, New York, 1989.

Parkinson, C. Northcote, *Parkinson's Law and Other Studies In Administration,* Houghton Mifflin Company, Boston, 1957.

Penzias, Arno, *Ideas and Information: Managing in a High-Tech World,* W. W. Norton & Company, New York, 1989.

Peter, Dr. Laurence J., *The Peter Pyramid, Or, Will We Ever Get the Point,* William Morrow Company, Inc., New York, 1986.

Peters, Thomas J. and Robert H. Waterman, Jr., *In Search of Excellence,* Warner Books, New York, 1982.

Peters, Tom, *Thriving On Chaos,* Harper & Row, New York, 1987.

Peters, Tom and Austin, Nancy, *A Passion for Excellence,* Random House, New York, 1985.

Pinchot III, Gifford, *Intrapreneuring,* Harper & Row, New York, 1985.

Polanyi, Karl, *The Great Transformation,* Beacon Press, Boston, 1944.

Poundstone, William, *Prisoner's Dilemma: John von Neumann, Game Theory, and the Puzzle of the Bomb*, Doubleday, New York, 1992.

Prigogine, Iiya and Stegners, Isabelle, *Order Out Of Chaos*, Bantam Books, Toronto, 1984.

Reedy, George E., *The Presidency In Flux*, Columbia University Press, New York, 1973.

Reich, Robert B., *The Next American Frontier*, Penguin Books, Ltd., New York, 1983.

Rifkin, Jeremy with Howard, Ted, *Entropy*, Bantam Books, Toronto, 1980.

Rifkin, Jeremy, *Time Wars*, Henry Holt and Company, New York, 1987.

Safire, William and Leonard Safir, *Leadership*, A Fireside book, Simon & Schuster, Inc., New York, 1990.

Sampson, Anthony, *Empires of the Sky*, Random House, New York, 1984.

Sampson, Anthony, *The Money Lenders*, Penguin Books, Ltd., Middlesex, 1981.

Schumacher, E. F., *Small is Beautiful*, Harper & Rowe Publishing, 1973.

Schwartz, Peter, *The Art of the Long View*, Doubleday Currency, New york, 1991.

Senge, Peter M. *The Fifth Discipline*, Doubleday Currency, New York, 1990.

Shurkin, Joel, *Engines of the Mind*, Pocket Books, New York, 1985.

Smith, Douglas K. and Alexander, Robert C., *Fumbling the Future*, William Morrow and Company, Inc., New York, 1988.

Starr, Paul, *The Social Transformation of American Medicine*, Basic Books, Inc., New York, 1982.

Tannen, Deborah, Ph.D., *You Just Don't Understand: Women and Men in Conversation*, Morrow Books, William Morrow & Company, New York City, New York, 1990.

Thurow, Lester C., *Dangerous Currents*, Random House, New York, 1983.

Thurow, Lester C., *The Zero-Sum Society*, Penguin Books, Ltd., Middlesex, 1980.

Thurow, Lester C., *The Zero-Sum Solution*, Simon and Schuster, Inc., New York, 1985.

Tichy, Noel M. and Devanna, Mary Anne, *The Transformational Leader*, John Wiley & Sons, New York, 1987.

Toffler, Alvin and Heidi Toffler, *PowerShift: Knowledge, Wealth, and Violence at the Edge of the 21st Century*, Bantom Books, 1990.

Tregoe, Benjamin B. John W. Zimmerman, Ronald A. Smith, Peter M. Tobia, *Vision and Action: Putting A Winning Strategy to Work*, Simon & Schuster, Inc. New York, 1989.

Tregoe, Benjamin B. and Zimmerman, John W., *Top Management Strategy*, Touchstone Book published by Simon & Schuster Inc, New York, 1980.

Tuchman, Barbara W., *A Distant Mirror*, Ballantine Books, New York, 1978.

Tuchman, Barbara W., *The Proud Tower*, The Macmillan Company, New York, 1965.

United States Bureau of the Census, *Statistical Abstract of the United States: 1982-83*, (103rd Edition), Washington, 1980.

von Oech, Roger, *A Whack On the Side of the Head*, Warner Books, Inc., New York, 1983.

von Hippel, Eric, *The Sources of Innovation*, Oxford University Press, New York, 1988.

von Oech, Roger, *A Kick In the Seat of the Pants*, Harper & Row, New York, 1986.

Walton, Mary, *The Deming Management Method*, The Putnam Publishing Group, New York, 1986.

Waterman, Robert H. Jr., *The Renewal Factor*, Bantam Books, Toronto, 1987.

Weaver, Paul H., *The Suicidal Corporation*, Simon and Schuster, Inc., New York, 1988.

Wiener, Norbert, *I Am A Mathematician*, The M.I.T. Press, Cambridge, 1956.

Will, George F., *Men At Work*, Macmillan Publishing Company, New York, 1990.

Wilson, James Q., *Bureaucracy - What Government Agencies Do and Why they Do It*, Basic Books, Harper Collins Publishers, 1989.

Wishy, Bernard, *The Child and the Republic*, University Press, Philadelphia, 1968.

Yergin, Daniel, *The Prize*, Simon and Schuster, New York, 1991.

Zuboff, Shoshana, *In the Age of the Smart Machine*, Basic Books, Inc., New York, 1984.

Zukav, Gary, *The Dancing Wu Li Masters*, Bantam Books, Toronto, 1979.

Zukav, Gary, *The Seat of the Soul*, Simon and Schuster, Inc., New York, 1989.